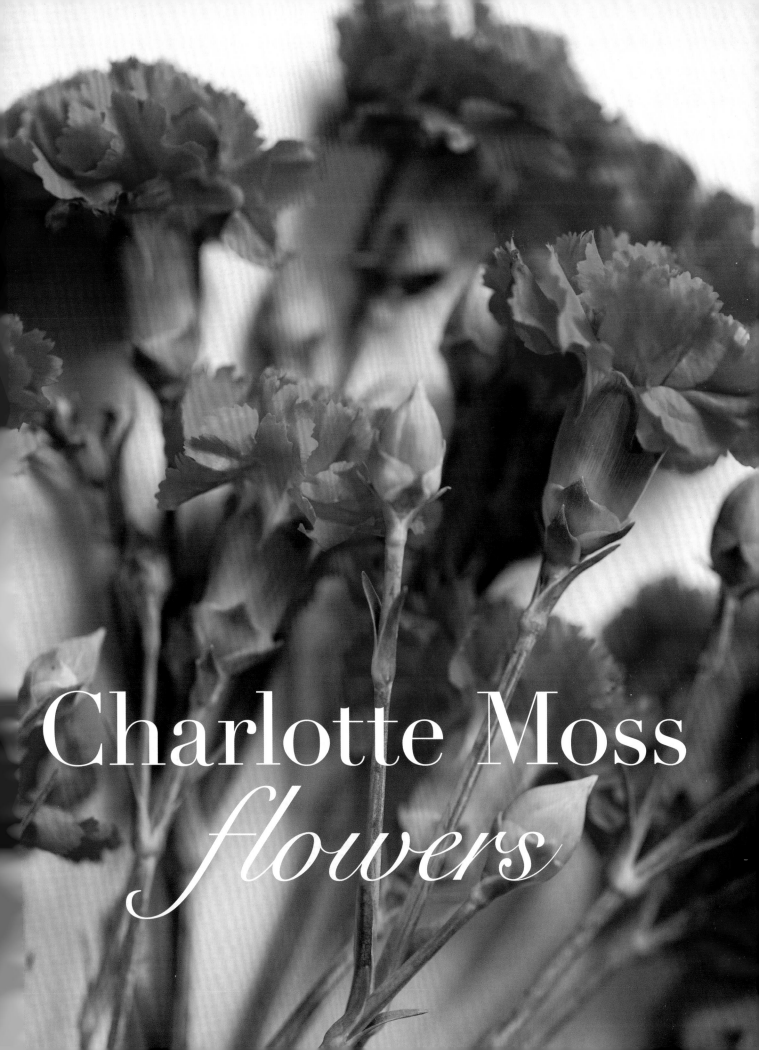

Charlotte Moss
flowers

Charlotte Moss

flowers

RIZZOLI NEW YORK

New York · Paris · London · Milan

CONTENTS

the power of a flower

*The creative urge is strong in us and among the
strong emotions of the human heart is
the love of beauty and a desire to create beauty.*

CONSTANCE SPRY

I BELIEVE THERE TO BE two schools of thought on the subject of flower arranging. I have studied the history of flower arranging, observed the work of those I admire, and have examined the work of the great flower painters—all the while practicing almost my entire adult life. Books and observation have been my silent, visual tutors.

As with much in life there is always a group that plays strictly by a book of rules burdened with preconception and concern for conformity. The get-out-the ruler-and-protractor-set, study-the-playbook-line-by-line manner of arranging inhibits spontaneity, experimentation, personalization, and, ultimately, joy. Then there are the ones who basically threw the rule book out the window. I would be part of that group. I have not always been the rebellious type, but when it comes to creative endeavors, I need breathing room. Flower arranging should be a joyous activity, something to look forward to and which provide hours of pleasure. It should not be fraught with anxiety and nail biting. I do understand some people get worked up. There is no test to be passed, no jury to examine, just you. So, if you are from the former school, perhaps you tuck that rule book away and just let the flowers tell you where they want to be. Books and rules are good to guide you, but they should not dictate. Having said all of that, if you need a book or two to guide you, take a look at the booklist on pages 264–67 that I have put together from my own library.

THE GARDEN IN JUNE

...wering of the Columbine is the beginning ...
... Tulips and Double Narcissi and stra...
...es may still afford bright colour or swee...
...e, but they do not charm us any longer, fo...
...of the spring, and the spring is past. What a
...old flower it is—"the Columbine commendable,"
...on called it four hundred years ago! Indeed,
...d garden writers mention it, its vigour and grace
...lways earned it a secure place in the English
...where it has been grown for centuries "for the
...oth of its form and colours." The Columbines
...ncestors were all varieties of the wild English
...*Aquilegia vulgaris*), and so vigorous and hand-
...some of these plants become under garden
...on, that it is questionable if any of the newer
...rpass them in beauty. However, the various
...f Aquilegia which have from time to time been
...o our garden flora are to be counted with the
...uable of plants, among the best of them being
...curiously coloured red and orange species known
...*nneri*, the tall golden *A. chrysantha*, and, perhaps
...utiful of all, the Rocky Mountain Columbine,
...a, with its quaint green "horns of honey."

Rules on volume, composition, shape, color, and suitable containers tend to make me squirm. All I want to do is gather my basket and shears, head to the garden, snip, and head to the flower room with whatever moved me. Similarly, in the city, at the florist or our local market, picking up what appeals is when the fun begins. Over time and with practice you will develop your own style, learn what works together, which flowers require the tall vase, which ones like breathing space. All of this, let me repeat, *all of this*, comes with practice and trial and error. Beware of too much thinking; give your instincts a chance.

Flowers have personalities. Tulips prefer vases straight up and down for support so they can continue to grow as they do. Small flowers, such as violets, often require bundling so they stay together in a vase like a nosegay, a bearded iris sometimes just wants to be alone, while roses, the queens of the garden, can do just about anything they want. What does all this mean, this flower talk? It means: relax, have fun, let your eye and the flowers guide you. Remember, they are flowers, one of mother nature's most glorious and ethereal creations. We marvel at the range of varieties, the colors, their grace, and their fragility. If you have a garden, you are sensitive to each flower and its idiosyncrasies. Maybe that gives you a head start over the non-gardener, but on the other hand, by making friends with the local florists, visiting their shops, and asking questions you will learn not only about the flowers but also, perhaps, some tricks of the trade. In addition to books and, of course, firsthand experience, there are blogs and beautiful Instagram accounts that share expertise, creativity, and a variety of beauty. If you want to learn, you have a wealth of resources just a click away.

PAGE 7 The flower room in New York City. OPPOSITE *Books on flowers, historic gardens, personages, plants, and arranging—a number seen here in East Hampton.*

I think about the countless museums I have visited in my life and the number of paintings that have drawn me in. Many of those paintings have been of flowers. In museums around the United States, from the Norton Simon to the Metropolitan, and in numerous iterations from around the globe, from the hieroglyphics in Egypt with lotus blossoms and palm trees, the carnations and tulips of Iznik tiles and ceramics in Istanbul and the delicate wall paintings at Herculaneum and Oplontis: so many memorable sights. I can think of countless examples of floral decoration in cloisonné, micromosaics, porcelains, bas relief, the marquetry of French furniture, and the *lacca povera* perfected by the Italians. Flower memories, near and far.

FLOWER MEMORIES

☘ Clover flowers, daisies, dandelions, and buttercups made great necklaces when I was seven. I loved the hours with cousins spent painstakingly threading them, with the reward of feeling bejeweled and dressed up. Necklace-making was a competitive sport back then—whose was the longest and the prettiest with the most flowers.

☘ On May Day in first grade all the girls in my class dressed in smocked frocks and danced around the maypole clutching a single lily in our hands. We did as we were told, I guess it was fun, I can't remember anything but the smell of the lilies. The power of a flower.

☘ As a teenager, I remember gathering "running cedar" in the woods on trail rides to bring back and watching my mother whip up some green magic—decorations for our house such as wreaths and topiaries; whatever it was, it made everything at home look prettier, fancier, more festive.

☘ At other times I would take plastic cups on those rides, praying to discover wild lady slipper orchids in the woods. One solitary pink blossom to bring home. I can smell them right now.

☘ I remember the blanket of wild violets that covered the ground around my grandfather's beagle house and my grandmother's rows of violet, brown, and amber-colored bearded iris, and the pink crape myrtle that dusted the driveway with their pink "snow."

☘ Some of these flower memories transport me to an age of innocence, a carefree time where days at the river began with pancakes and ended with ice cream while sitting on the pier. In between, I remember lounging on the large floral-printed bark cloth cushions sitting on my grandmother's deep ruby-colored wicker.

☘ Do you remember the first time you wore a boutonniere or a corsage? Who gave it to you, what was the occasion, what were you wearing? Was it a dance, a prom, a wedding? Another rite of passage into adulthood where flowers paved the way. Do you remember the first time someone arrived at your front door with a flower delivery and it was for *you*? The excitement of it all, the anticipation opening the card! Or when a bouquet arrived at your office and everyone gathered around to hear who it was from? I remember how important those moments

From my travel diary. CLOCKWISE FROM TOP LEFT *Hieroglyphics in an ancient temple in Egypt. | Detail of trompe-l'oeil murals in the Bergl Rooms at Schönbrunn Palace, Vienna, Austria, painted by Johann Wenzel Bergl at the request of Empress Maria Theresa. | Delicately carved flowers in marble at the Taj Mahal, India. | Frescoed wall decoration at Oplontis, Italy, executed before the eruption of Mount Vesuvius in 79 AD, and preserved underground until rediscovered in the nineteenth century.*

were, those "flower firsts." Although I must admit I have few recollections of specific flowers or the person, aside from a school dance or two.

❧ Scroll forward. Who could forget the songs of the 1960s summoning you: "If you're going to San Francisco, be sure to wear some flowers in your hair." I am sure I wore a ring of flowers in my hair to some outdoor concert back then, but I didn't make it to San Francisco until later. We were flower children then, espousing peace and love. Who didn't want more peace and more love? *Plus ça change . . .*

❧ I remember the floor-through apartment I shared with three women during my senior year of college. Every once in a while, one of those straw-wrapped Chianti bottles got repurposed as a vase. Maybe that's when I realized that anything can be a vase and that it only takes a few blossoms to perk up a room.

❧ Years later, I remember I bought some flowers for my office on Wall Street. A small windowless space with regulation-issue corporate furniture, white walls, and industrial-strength carpet; it needed help. I remember a great shop in Greenwich Village where I bought two baskets for my in- and out-boxes. They were beautiful and a little out of my budget, but I thought they were elegant. Next came a simple vase

ABOVE Works of art are a constant inspiration. Here: Frédéric Bazille, Young Woman with Peonies, 1870. OPPOSITE A sampling of arrangements.

with flowers. After installing those three items, which I thought would be the most the office could handle, it was business as usual. Until two male stockbrokers came in and "for my own good" informed me that no one was going to take me seriously now; my new additions were not very corporate. Poor souls that they were . . . I wonder where they are now? Torturing a wife somewhere, micromanaging her attempts to make things better, prettier, happier. Maybe that was one of the turning points in my life, the moment I realized I was not long for that world. I am so glad to be writing *this* book rather than one on liquid yield option notes.

❧ I will never forget my first trip to Chatsworth with the American Friends of the Georgian Group, which was just getting started in the United States. After lunch and touring some of the house with Deborah ("Debo"), then Duchess of Devonshire, we went to explore the gardens, past the cascade, the Paxton

greenhouses, the famous Willow Tree Fountain, and on to the lupine garden. Never have I ever seen, or seen since, such a display of lupines in all their glory. The rainbow palette of blossoms standing almost human-sized, as if they anticipated our visit. That image remains so clear. The power of a flower.

❧ Once you have been to Sissinghurst witnessing its white garden at its peak, you've reached a pinnacle. Knowing its history and origin as a ruin, nothing can compare. Sissinghurst is gardening mecca.

❧ My visit to Château de Chenonceau in the Loire Valley is memorable for a number of reasons. Its rich history, the gallery over the bridge that connects the

ABOVE Lupines, photographed during a visit to Chatsworth in the late 1980s. OPPOSITE Details of the garden at Sissinghurst, the result of a true gardening marriage. Harold Nicolson created the plan while his wife, Vita Sackville-West, the romanticist, put meat on its bones—she was the one who knew flowers.

château to the other side of the River Cher, and the flowers in the rooms open to the public. Somewhere in my pile of photos is a picture of a delicate basket filled with *fraises de bois* trained over a miniature trellis sitting on a seventeenth-century oak table. I will never forget it. This fragile fruit, supported as if espaliered, was a little wonder that would have inspired Fabergé.

❧ On the opening night of the Chelsea Flower Show—one of many visits to this floral extravaganza in London—my husband and I were in a marquee sponsored by his bank. I think it took a couple of British bankers to convince this American banker that the opening night, when the Queen visits the show, is *the* night *tout le monde* attends. My husband, somewhat skeptical, asked my opinion. Of course I emphatically answered *yes*. As we walked through one of the exhibition stands that evening, my husband heard his name being called. He turned to find the chairman of the Bank of England standing under a bower of David Austin roses. Never again did those bankers ever have to convince him that a flower show in London was an important corporate event. The power of a flower.

❧ Arriving at a dinner party in Paris in a beautiful and romantic *hôtel particulier*—the mural-wrapped entry gallery illuminated by candlelight—was the dramatic beginning of the evening. Dinner guests walked down a stone gallery, turning slightly to descend stone steps. The portieres on either side of the entry screened the surprise around the corner, but the fragrance announced roses. There, on two large, skirted, and *objet*-filled round tables were large baskets with rosebushes in full bloom. Garden roses in a perfect state of voluptuousness gently staked with bamboo and tied neatly with raffia, they stood six feet tall. I can't remember my dinner partner that evening, but the roses I will never forget.

In colors of sapphire, topaz, and amber, the irises at Parc de Bagatelle in their brief moment of glory are a flower lover's dream.

16 CHARLOTTE MOSS FLOWERS

On another visit to France my husband and I arrived early one morning and were driven to the Beaujolais region for our stay at the Château de Bagnols. Upon arrival, still half asleep from the trip, we followed the gentleman with our luggage through a covered passageway to the château. Suddenly, I was awakened by a powerful fragrance. But where and what? Then it hit me: lavender. It was lavender, but where? Then I looked up. The entire ceiling of the passage was covered with bundles of lavender hanging to dry. I knew this was a very good sign for our visit; my expectations were now duly heightened. The lavender could have hung in any number of places at a large château, but the selection of that spot to greet and seduce was perfection.

Irises are some of my earliest flower memories. The tall bearded iris variety that my grandmother had in her garden in Virginia. I mostly remember the unusual palette; I had never seen flowers that were brown, amber, and blue. I assumed these were rare specimens that my grandmother obtained somewhere, because most gardens I had seen up to that point were explosions of yellows and oranges, and reds mixed with pinks and purples. I also remember that when she picked them, her bouquet seemed stingy to me at the time; three, maybe five stems. I know I never asked her "Why not more?" because she was my grandmother and like most children I just assumed she knew all. Besides, I did not have a clue back then about such concepts as simplicity and restraint. Now I see that that thing I called stinginess is simple elegance. One graceful stem of a bearded iris with its tissue paper petals *is* an arrangement.

An allée of laburnum at Haseley Court, in the garden created by Nancy Lancaster, with a spiderweb bench inviting one to sit and enjoy it all.

Years later, on what would be one of many visits to the Petit Hameau at Versailles, I noticed irises growing along the rooflines of the thatched structures, a curiously beautiful and puzzling sight. My research later revealed that these flowers—a low-growing variety from Japan called *iris tectorum*—actually prolong the life of a thatch roof, thriving there while absorbing excess water. As the story goes, this dainty creature ended up on rooftops in Japan after a long-ago emperor declared land to be too valuable for growing flowers in a postwar era. Hence, up to the rooftops they went.

Fast forward, and once again in France, I was visiting the horticultural school at Château de Chaumont in the Loire Valley, as well as the flower show at Château de Courson, with my sister Cathy. It was May, and gardens everywhere were competing for the attention of gardeners and tourists. We were returning to Paris in the late afternoon, and I asked our driver, Henner, to make a detour to Parc de Bagatelle because we were only minutes away. While it was too early in the season for the display of roses there, it was the perfect time of day, the golden hour, to experience the place. The bearded irises were at their peak, with the beautiful light dancing from bed to bed and the blossoms proudly standing shoulder to shoulder. Every once in a while, the light caught the luminous petals, transforming them into sapphires, amethysts, and golden amber. In this intimate enclosure there were only a few people, and we waited patiently for them to leave. Then, we had the entire garden to ourselves. That time I can only describe as being something close to what heaven must be like. I have never seen an iris garden like that since and consider myself lucky for having been there at that magical moment. It was then that I made the promise to myself to make time for irises in my life. To do my homework, select varieties, and do what my grandmother did years ago. There is more work to be done, and there are more varieties to collect, more flowers to be enjoyed.

❧ Decades later, the challenge of childhood necklace-making has been replaced with decorating, gardening, and entertaining. Traveling to places far and near has afforded opportunities to observe beauty in more ways than I imagined possible. These quests have been solo, as well as in the company of kindred spirits—old friends and new, and as luck would have it, all with similar interests and points of view. Simultaneous sighs while experiencing display gardens at London's Chelsea Flower Show, the brilliant yellow of the laburnum tunnel at Haseley Court, the Chinese Room at Kelmarsh Hall, and the Saloon at Ditchley Park decorated with urns of flowers and candlelit with tables set for dinner—our own.

❧ Scroll back a few years, when I called Margot Shaw and proposed putting a group together to see Nancy Lancaster's three houses in England. Phone calls back and forth; invitations extended; Indagare, our travel advisor, engaged; and date set. We stayed at Ditchley Park, venturing on private tours of the other houses and gardens, places that Lancaster created on English soil with her indomitable American spirit and highly evolved instinct for all things beautiful. Lancaster would herself claim that she was "always searching for beauty." Her three essentials for a successful room have become the mantra of her disciples: a fire, candlelight, and flowers.

❧ Beautiful houses, châteaux, gardens—there are so many more memorable visits, but there was a particular moment that really touched me. While in London on a buying trip for my store years ago, I found myself stopped dead in traffic on the Gloucester Road. (In the days before mobile phones, people were more keenly focused on their surroundings than what appeared on a tiny screen.) After a moment, I looked up at the second-floor window of a large brick Victorian building. There on the windowsill sat five green Perrier bottles, each holding a tulip. I grabbed my camera and snapped that shot. An image I can see today, where someone recycled five bottles with as many tulips to make their own statement of beauty. How easy it was to make that view prettier for them and the lucky passersby. I have used that slide in numerous lectures I have given. The act was so simple, the message very powerful.

These memories were the beginning of a long path to a world filled with observing, admiring, emulating, and attempting to create beauty—oftentimes with flowers.

I could continue on with flower memories and in fact more may surface throughout this book. I am not one for nostalgia, but it's difficult to write about this subject without the thread of memory that compelled me to start recalling them in the first place. Flower power.

This book began its life literally as a diary of the ten-plus years I have spent documenting flower arrangements in two houses. Never did I think the

OPPOSITE, CLOCKWISE FROM TOP LEFT A footed basket filled with garden roses on the living room mantel in East Hampton. | Dinner in the garden in New York City, a tablescape of delicate petunia-filled baskets. | A mixed arrangement of Japanese anemones, roses, hydrangeas, astrantia, and greens—all from the garden—in a basket from Colefax & Fowler. | The famous saloon at Ditchley Park, decorated for dinner during my visit there.

FLOWER ARRANGEMENTS

documentation would become a book, because the record-keeping was just for myself and shot mostly with a digital camera and an iPhone. Ten years on, I have accumulated masses of photographs recording hundreds of arrangements.

In a meeting one day with my publisher Charles Miers and my editor Philip Reeser, I described a couple of potential books. When I said we could do a book on flowers that would be primarily images, Charles immediately and characteristically quipped, "Charlotte, you cannot do a book with mostly photos. That's not in your DNA. You are a teacher, and it's too important for you that readers learn something, that they have useful takeaways."

So, as Charles predicted, here we are, in the expanded and hopefully improved version of my first proposal, a record of some of those arrangements, some "takeaways" as Charles would say, and a little history through the eyes of some notable women who made flowers an integral part of their lives. So much has been written about the lives of these women, but here I have chosen to focus on one shared passion. In the French countryside, London, New York, and Virginia, all pursued very different lives, but each one, either in her own home or in those of others, left behind a trail of that ephemeral thing we call style. All flowers were embraced, including the weeds in the field and along the roadside, and the outliers on the lawn. At first glance, the women featured here may seem like a rather disparate group, but one common thread is their embrace of beauty. Each of these women spent a lifetime pursuing beauty, singing its virtues, creating it in their own private universe and for the world at large.

For years I have been documenting my flower diary, cataloguing my flower arrangements, and mounting the photographs in handmade books.

Most importantly they created to please themselves. The natural, mixed bouquets of Gertrude Jekyll; the wild, woolly, tour-de-force combinations of Constance Spry; the omnipresence of flower arrangements, floral fabrics, and botanical art in the residences of Lee Radziwill. Each of these women contributed to a floral legacy in which anyone can find inspiration. Their unique styles, the result of instinct and intuition, coupled with study, confidence, and discipline, have collectively left us a visual handbook to guide us, to nurture us, and to inspire us.

This is not a history book. If it does, however, pique your interest in history in any way, start with the booklist at the back of this book. I recall some of my first books purchased in the 1970s. Later, in the '80s, while traveling to England and France on a regular basis, I picked up books not only in bookstores but also at antiques shops, flea markets, country fairs, museum shops, and auctions. Most libraries grow slowly over time and require editing every now and then. Be patient with your acquisitions so that each one will take on greater meaning.

I have learned many things while arranging flowers. I have learned to trust my own instincts, to shake off preconceived notions about the proper ways to do things, and to be open-minded, as anything that can be plucked from anywhere can find its way into a vase. I have experimented and continue to do so, and I have continued to collect anything that might enjoy life as a vase. I have learned by reading about how others do things, I have visited flower gardens and collections, and I have studied books and paintings, but most of all I have just enjoyed getting to know my flowers and observing how they like to be arranged. The *power* of a flower. ❀

at home
with flowers

CITY & COUNTRY

CHAPTER I

New York

*A woman's environment will speak for her life, whether
she likes it or not. . . . A house is a dead giveaway.*

ELSIE DE WOLFE, *The House in Good Taste*

BECAUSE I WAS RAISED IN THE SOUTH, adjusting to life in New York
City took some doing. Taxis, subways, all the small shops it took visiting—
the wine shop, the cheese shop (of course), the grocery store—just to have
dinner guests. And then learning where to buy plants and flowers! Mind you,
most of this was done with individual trips because I was not loading up a car
in those days, which were the late 1970s. Today, car services and Uber driv-
ers help facilitate things for some; but back then, it was an aerobic workout.
Every neighborhood has its merchants, and then there are the places one
must seek out because they are unusual or fabulous and not to be missed.
Thank goodness for Zezé Flowers and Plaza Flowers for arrangements and
beautiful flowers to compose your own, and mainstays of New York's Flower
District, such as Dutch Flower Line for anything and everything; Milton for
topiary; G. Page for endless flowers; Holiday Flower and Plant for orchids,
ferns, trees, and shrubs; and US Evergreen for everything that spells holiday
for the exterior and interior of the house. Then there's always a stop at Jamali
to see what's new in containers. I couldn't live without this flower family to
make it all happen at home.

I don't grow flowers in the city, therefore knowing where to go for fresh supplies and who specializes in what economizes my time. If I can block out time on a Monday morning, a trip to the flower market can jump-start the week. The abundance of material, the colors, the energy, the smells—it is inspiring stimulation for the senses. I love exploring the neighborhood markets, just to see what's on the street and in the shops. Sometimes you go with an idea; other times you let what's available do all the talking. Ideas can sometimes create blinders, inhibiting your vision, because you are so focused on a specific mission. That's not to say that an idea is a bad thing by any means; it's just that in the case of a beautiful flower market, you want to take in the beauty and allow yourself to be inspired by what's around you.

One thing you can count on in every neighborhood in New York is the local grocery market or deli with a flower stand on the sidewalk. In season, they are well stocked with daffodils, tulips, sunflowers, hydrangeas, lilies, mixed bunches, and more. Having flowers at home is made that much easier, especially if you are the single-flower arranging sort. It may sound trite, but flowers around the house really do have a way of bringing the garden indoors; and absent a garden, it's even more important.

At home, flowers at my bedside are a must. All of us have our priorities and idiosyncrasies—this is one of mine. They are the first thing I see in the morning and the last thing I see before bedtime, along with a book and a husband, that is.

Having flowers in the entry vestibule is a great welcome for guests and for the family every day. It is how I choose to be welcomed back home after a day at the office or a business trip. Farther on, in the front hall, I like something on the commode from time to time, as the spirit moves me. Nearby there are two French enameled jardinières that are always filled with plants.

In the library, where I spend a lot of time, there are flowers next to my reading chair and on the mantel when something inspires. And just as the flowers of each season change, so do things in and around the house. A bowl of persimmons and bittersweet vine one week might be replaced by a silver vase filled with shades of maroon flowers and leaves, and next by the blue-and-white cachepots with white dahlias.

Flowers bring beauty into our lives, and color, fragrance, and life to our rooms and, in a way, they challenge us to make the most of every day. ❧

CHAPTER 2

East Hampton

There's a charming two-word rule for flowers,
given to me by Beverley Nichols, the noted gardener and author.
He said, "Love them." I recommend these words to you.

FLEUR COWLES

HOUSES SHOULD, AS Vita Sackville-West wrote, "be of the country, not in the country"—a critical nuance that describes how a house is theoretically married to its surroundings. Our house in East Hampton sits quietly at the end of a road that terminates in a bridle path, a public easement, so there is no through traffic. It is quiet and private, and creates our patch of country. Houses and gardens have a *sotto voce* manner of prescribing a lifestyle that reflects their surroundings—we have long since comfortably settled into ours.

Years ago I wrote a book called *Winter House* (2005). This book was not only about our house in Aspen but also a celebration of the season that we primarily spent there: Thanksgiving, Christmas, and some late-season skiing. It was a cozy, European alpine-style house on a quiet street nicely nestled in town, with views up the mountains where all activities reflected what the landscape had to offer. Houses have a way of communicating with their surroundings and their inhabitants, almost like a bridge connecting us with the natural environment.

I'll light the fire.
You place the flowers in the
vase that you bought today.

GRAHAM NASH

In East Hampton we celebrate summer and every other moment we can spend there. In the beginning of the season we impatiently watch color in the garden making its entrance. In the middle we luxuriate in an abundance of blooms, and in the end I reluctantly gather every last flower to compose my "last gasp" arrangement. East Hampton is our "summer" house and every arrangement here reflects what's available in the garden, as well as at the farmers market, at roadside stands, at nurseries, and from Annie at Sag Harbor Florist, from whom I get a weekly list of floral offerings. Here, it is impossible to be without flowers throughout the house—from the large arrangements in the front hall that greet everyone and into the living room where the mantel and side tables become alternating display opportunities. Small vases are placed on book tables in the living room and in the powder room. The breakfast table always has a cluster of vases—a single stem, a bunch of herbs, basically anything that is available. As anyone who loves arranging knows, there is always a casualty or two, stems that bend or break, but even those are put into miniature vases on the shelves of the flower room.

In the summer we enjoy most of our evening meals on the garden room porch, where the table always has a centerpiece. The dining room table usually has a landscape of antique porcelain vegetables, some by Lady Anne Gordon, and a central cabbage tureen by Vladimir Kanevsky.

One of the great pleasures, of course, is to create something for houseguests, and I always select a special vase for a fragrant bedside bouquet.

Every weekend I spend time in my flower room—fussing, arranging, photographing, and relaxing. Just being there selecting a vase, listening to music, and quietly composing an arrangement: it's like telling a story with flowers, and each one has a happy ending. ❧

Flowers are the paint box of garden design.

BUNNY MELLON

PART II
flower diary

flower diary

*There is only one "basic rule" in flower arrangement.
And that is to love the flowers, to listen to what
they have to say, to watch the way they dance, and then
to allow them to express themselves in their own sweet way.*

BEVERLEY NICHOLS, *The Art of Flower Arrangement*

THE GARDEN CLUB OF AMERICA has done much to elevate the art of flower arranging, since its establishment in the 1910s, by creating local chapters, providing education, and holding competitions. The flower shows on the local and national level have proven that there is a strong interest in learning and doing, demonstrating that anyone can express themselves through the collection and assembly of a few stems and leaves.

Anyone striving to advance their skills and learn more about the how and what—whether using material sourced from gardens, fields, forest, or flower shops—has an enormous bank of information and tools at their fingertips today. Literally at the press of a button, you can watch demonstrations and attend lectures and flower shows online. You can watch YouTube videos and search hashtags on Instagram for beautiful and personal examples.

Flower arranging, or what Constance Spry called "doing the flowers," is quite a democratic pursuit. You can spend as little or as much as you like, combine that with your sense of color, your eye for scale and proportion, all laced with a little creativity, and you are on your way—and never discount a little improvisation here and there. ❦

A FEW THOUGHTS ON
FLOWER ARRANGING

HERE ARE A FEW PRACTICAL thoughts for you, things that I have learned over the years from reading and a whole lot of trial and error. I'm sure you have your own to add—if not now, then surely later.

✤ What comes first, the flowers or the vase? It depends! If, for example, you are filling a tureen of flowers for the dining table, the size of that container will guide your selection of blossoms, just as a special table setting (the plates, the linens, the flatware) may direct your color choice. On the other hand, you may pass a market or go to a florist and come home with tulips that require support, hence a tall vase; a bunch of daisies may call out for a basket or a white ceramic cachepot; or a nosegay of violets might require something short. It all comes with time, practice, and an open mind.

✤ Just about anything that holds water can hold flowers, so keep an open mind when you are shopping; and for heaven's sake shop your own cupboards. There is always something that has been long forgotten that has interesting possibilities.

✤ As flowers can be short- and tall-stemmed, some leafless and others quite leafy (to name just a few variables), their characteristics should guide your selection of a vase. With experience you will learn and it will be become second nature.

✤ Keep a selection of flower frogs, which help arrange and steady blossoms. Frogs come in metal, glass, and ceramic. I would suggest having a few of each for different vessels and types of flowers.

✤ You have seen florists use florist tape on a wide-mouth vase or a bowl. This support is another solution, used particularly if the vase is glass and the frog would be visible, which might not be desirable.

✤ There are lots of flower shears available. Try them out in your hand first to make sure they are comfortable for you. No one wants a blister or a sore hand from trimming flowers with an improper instrument. The same goes for secateurs, which I use to cut stems and branches in the garden.

✤ I love the flexibility of chicken wire for positioning flowers in a vase. It can be cut to size, shaped, and used again and again. Beware of the edges, which can be sharp!

✤ I use two different types of gloves when working on my arrangements. Gardening gloves from Foxgloves come in soft knits and washable suedes for working with most any blooms *except* roses. Because a number of roses have absolutely wicked thorns, I use Pine Tree gloves for those occasions; they are thicker and feature a rubberized material that makes it more difficult for thorns to penetrate.

❧ Every once in a while there are those unruly stems that need a touch of discipline. Tying stems together lightly with twine, raffia, or raffia-wrapped wire can be the solution. These materials will help keep flowers in place in your vase.

❧ Just before you pitch something into the recycling bin, give it a second thought as a potential liner for a vase or basket. Plastic water bottles (both round and square) and take-out food containers are all possibilities. I have a collection that gets employed regularly. Baskets always need a liner, but I also like using light plastic as protection for inside my antique containers. To lengthen the life span of your flowers, throw your liners in the dishwasher, which will keep them clean and free of bacteria.

❧ Stem strippers are simple plastic devices that facilitate the removal of unwanted leaves and rose thorns from stems.

❧ Bottle brushes are the best tools to clean containers by getting into those hidden corners and reaching the bottoms of tall vases.

❧ Use a plastic or galvanized-metal bucket full of water to plunge flowers into right after cutting and prior to arranging to keep them fresh. This step will give you a chance to get organized, make your vase selection, and contemplate your arrangement.

❧ Think clean: clean vases, clean buckets, clean scissors.

❧ Continue watering your arrangements. The first day, freshly cut flowers will drink a lot. Check the water level at the end of the day and top up the water. Sometimes I change water in clear glass containers for appearances. It depends on the flowers; some are just messier than others.

❧ Misting your arrangements lightly has a way of giving them a dewy look, and it hydrates them in drier climates. Take arrangements to the kitchen for this to prevent damaging furniture or spotting wallpaper.

❧ A drop cloth or a sheet of plastic can be useful to collect leaves and stems while cutting, and to protect a workspace or the floor.

So much has been said on this subject, so I'm stopping here. Take a look at the booklist, on pages 264–67, that I have put together from my library, which includes some of my favorite books on the how-to's of arranging, flowers in general, and visual lessons from some of the pros in the business. Don't stop here, carry on.

CHAPTER 3

Flower Room

I am not what I am,
I am what I do with my hands.

LOUISE BOURGEOIS

IT DOESN'T MATTER whether you have a room, a shed, a closet, or a table, as long as you have a place to call your own when it comes to arranging flowers for your home. A dedicated space or real estate commandeered from the kitchen, mudroom, or garage will do. A place to store the necessities is key to organization: vases, clippers, watering can, frogs, chicken wire—all the basics within reach.

A surface space large enough for a lazy Susan—allowing you to rotate your in-process creations—ensures that your arrangements have balance. Such a simple thing facilitates your flower arranging and helps to avoid those "bed-head" bouquets.

We could fill volumes with how-to advice when it comes to arranging flowers but, as I have said before, I did not set out to write a how-to because there are so many available titles that specifically contain that information, and I have listed many in the back of this one. From the exuberance of Constance Spry to the restraint of ikebana, from the fussiness of the Victorians to the clean lines of midcentury modernism, flower styles seem to parallel decoration and clothing fashions. I would encourage anyone to find a book with the style you are drawn to, then practice, practice, practice. That's what I do every week.

Years ago, I wrote a piece on the potting shed at Madoo Conservancy in Sagaponack, near my home in East Hampton. I interviewed the late Robert

Dash, artist, raconteur, writer, and creator of the garden. Bob created Madoo from nothing, and I mean nothing—it was a field, a dirt field. I assumed he was channeling Harold Nicolson and Vita Sackville-West at Sissinghurst, the holy grail of gardening they created from ruins amidst mountains of dust. Fast forward to today, and Madoo is one of our local treasures on the East End of Long Island. Bob was quick when it came to doling out advice that day and, for that matter, he was pretty good at doing it every day, solicited or not.

On that day the specific question was about potting sheds. How they could be organized for flower arranging and potting readiness. The same applies to any flower room, or space you choose to work in where there is an expectation of productivity. Bob responded, "It will look like a mess, of course, if it is working well. If it is working well, it is laboratory, kitchen, nursery, training camp, military installation always on alert." Bob's sense of humor surfaced even as it related to his potting shed. Then, without missing a beat, he added, "And Champagne, always Champagne."

COLLECTING CONTAINERS

I have collected vases for a very long time. It would be embarrassing to take inventory and count, so I won't. What is unusual about a collection of vases is that you don't find yourself saying, "I think I'll go buy one today." That is just not how it happens. While antiques shopping, I might find one tucked in a corner; at a thrift shop I could score a stack of baskets; a friend sends me violets for my birthday in a beautiful silver cup; and now my stepson James Friedberg is making me beautiful glass containers in a variety of sizes and shapes. As I mentioned earlier, just about anything that can hold water, or accommodate something that will hold water, can be a vase.

When I am in my flower room with a basket of cut flowers, I scan the shelves asking myself, "What container today? What will work best with this bunch? What haven't I used in a while? Where are these flowers going?" I always imagine that all of my vases are vying for my attention, each one wondering who will get picked next, who will be paired with the centerpiece, the bedside nosegay, or the new entrance hall bouquet, greeter of all. The great thing about vases is they hold the promise of beauty to come.

If you have ever collected *anything*, you understand that a collection sometimes just happens. Your interest may have been sparked by something given to you as a gift, or perhaps something you stumbled upon in an antiques shop. Encouragement from parents and friends spurred you on to collect and learn more. Before you knew it, you had a collection. You start with one item, then another; then whatever it is magically finds you. Funny how that happens. How many times have you exclaimed while shopping, "It was just waiting for me"? More than once, I reckon. This is what happens to collectors.

In this case, we are talking vases. If you love flowers, grow flowers, or are the lucky recipient of flowers from time to time, you will want just the right vase to put them in. Which vase? One compatible with the room where the flowers are destined to be and, most importantly, one that complements the flowers themselves. Flower decoration is an ephemeral aspect of interior decoration, the last accessory to be added and the first to be removed and replaced regularly. It is the "branch" of decoration that presents multiple opportunities and that challenges us to keep things in a room fresh and inviting.

Flowers and their vessels are an important accessory that you will want to sync with the room, or perhaps create a signature look for yourself. It's something to ponder as you start honing your skills. Maybe the answer is simply glass in varying shapes and sizes, the simplicity of a single bud vase, or a porcelain bowl. Whatever it is, it is a place to begin.

Over the years. I have purchased vases from beautiful antiques shops here and in my travels to Europe and elsewhere. Catalogues, garden centers, studios of artisans and craftspeople, flea markets, thrift shops, and supermarkets are abundant hunting grounds. The containers I have in New York City tend to be more formal—porcelains, antique toles, silver and bronze—while East Hampton's stock is less formal. My collections of baskets and delft live there, along with rustic wooden buckets, enamels, ceramics—truthfully, a little bit of everything. There will always be overlap because, just as in decorating, I think contrasts are what enliven a room. Objects have a funny way of communicating, perking each other up and supporting each other. If you have ever taken the time to putter around the house and move things around, you no doubt have had those moments when you have stopped to remove something that has more or less had its day. Moving objects from room to room allows them to take on a new life elsewhere. Also, simply experimenting and rearranging everything on a table can be terribly gratifying. A new look with no expense: now there's a decorating concept for you.

By giving contrasts a chance, you will begin to realize that there is no rule book. Give your creativity a try and let your intuition guide you as you begin to develop a rapport with all of your materials at hand. A basket full of daisies on an Italian console, a small cluster of silver bud vases with single stems on a farmhouse table, or a Sèvres urn with grasses surrounded by candles on the dining room table. For your muse, look to passionately inventive floral designer Constance Spry, who used antique incense burners, tin cans, and gilded Empire urns as receptacles for her creations. Once again, the refrain: experiment, practice, and, most importantly, enjoy yourself. And remember, a vase holds a promise, a promise of something to come, a promise of beauty. ♣

*Do what you please,
follow your own star.
Just be natural and
gay and lighthearted
and pretty and simple
and overflowing and
general and baroque
and bare and austere
and stylized and
wile and daring and
conservative, and learn
and learn and learn.*

CONSTANCE SPRY

MUSE

Constance Spry

This joyful experience [of arranging flowers] is for everyone . . . who loves a beautiful thing and will take a little trouble.

CONSTANCE SPRY (1886–1960) was arguably the most gifted and influential floral artist of the last century. And yet, search for her on the internet, and you will find she is almost as well known for her invention of coronation chicken, served at Queen Elizabeth II's ascension to the throne in 1953. This is revealing both about the place of floral artistry in our culture and the wide range of Spry's talents.

Drawing inspiration as much from seventeenth-century Dutch floral paintings as from the roadside, vegetable patch, and country field, Spry was a true artist whose materials were from nature. She employed the diverse treasures of the natural world—such as seed heads, buds, catkins, weeds, dried grasses and leaves, winter berries, and even vegetable foliage—along with more conventional floral fare, in a way no one had before. By turning the bounty of nature into art, Spry enlarged our appreciation of its wonders and expanded our sense of the beautiful. "If ever history was written in flowers, she wrote it," noted Beverley Nichols of Spry in *The Art of Flower Arrangement* (1967).

Spry was born in England and had a humble upbringing in Ireland, escaping a bad first marriage and toggling for years between work as a civil servant and a teacher. With the help of her second husband, in 1929 she opened her first shop

in London, called simply "Flower Decoration." An arrangement she fashioned out of hedgerow flowers (in reality, weeds) for the window of a smart Old Bond Street perfumery caused a sensation in fashionable society. In 1934, she moved to a larger shop, founded the Constance Spry Flower School, both of which employed seventy people, and released her first book, also called *Flower Decoration*. By then, it was she who defined what was fashionable in society. She was called upon for the top events of the day, including the wedding of the Duke and Duchess of Windsor.

And yet Spry always remained connected to teaching and helping others. She was devoted to sharing her gifts with people from all walks of life, instructing teenage factory workers as well as country chatelaines. During the war, she lectured all over Britain and published *Come Into the Garden, Cook* to encourage Britons to grow their own food. After the war, she started a school with a friend to teach domestic arts. For Queen Elizabeth II's coronation, Spry did the flowers at Westminster Abbey and, with her students, catered a lunch for foreign delegates, serving their coronation chicken recipe.

In her many wonderful books, she delightfully shares her enthusiasm for "doing the flowers." Having flowers indoors was about enhancing one's home, rather than just creating a botanical display, so an arrangement's setting and container must be considered in tandem with the flowers one chooses.

She wants us to be open to "choose freely from whatever provides the shape and color one needs," without being inhibited by convention or prejudice. In this way, if you were making an arrangement in reds, you wouldn't just go into the garden looking for roses or dahlias, but you might begin to notice instead materials you had never thought of using: a spray of currant tomatoes, a branch of elderberry, or the ruddy inflorescence of a grass. And in doing this you probably would also have found a pleasing variety of contrasting shapes and textures to make your arrangement more interesting. Spry's goal in all of her many charmingly written books is to just "make suggestions and scatter ideas about." She wanted our imaginations to have free rein in the creation of these "living pictures."

Even if you live in the city, Spry advises on how to use flower shops and allotments, and how to collect when on holiday, or on an outing in the country, or even at the market. "There is decorative material to be found among the most ordinary vegetables; carrots, parsnip, and kale leaves, among others, take on glorious winter color." Indeed Nichols writes about Spry finding treasure—dead hydrangea heads—on her rubbish heap. Spry taught us to see; now it's up to us to look. ❧

PRECEDING PAGES Constance Spry, 1953. OPPOSITE Branches and stems, blooming or not, were part of the Constance Spry language of floral arranging.

CHAPTER 4

Single-Flower Arrangements

*I think that flowers in themselves are one of the
miracles of life. . . . I have a special passion for arranging them.
Every time it is as if you were painting a flower picture.*

KAREN BLIXEN

I AM SURE THAT, FOR SOME PEOPLE, creating an arrangement with only
one type of flower may not be considered arranging at all. The prospect of
assembling two dozen tulips or a bunch of sweet William or dahlias is certainly fraught with far less anxiety than the daunting task of creating a mixed
bouquet that honors the Dutch Masters.

Anxiety is not an ingredient you want in your flower arrangement; it
undermines your process, makes you second-guess yourself, and can be discouraging. We'll have none of that. Onward.

Back to your arrangement. Trimming off excess leaves (particularly below
the waterline), removing any grit, and trimming the bottoms of stems are
basically the prep you do with all your flowers. Your next step is to carefully
place each flower in your vase, one by one. Over time you will learn how
much to trim certain flowers, who likes to stand tall, who likes it tight and

*I shouldn't like
to go through life
without flowers . . .
they are a sign of
joy. . . . Flowers,
for me, are a
great source of
inspiration . . . they
bring happiness.*

VALENTINO

cozy in the vase, and that tulips will just do whatever the heck they want. Single-flower arrangements can be great confidence boosters, because the outcome is beautiful while the effort is minimal.

Experiment with different flowers and select small- to medium-sized containers before you move on to tackling larger urns and jardinières. Building confidence is the key to having your own style with flowers. Gloria Vanderbilt celebrated single-flower bouquets with her tulip fabrics for Bloomcraft in the 1970s. Other textiles were designed with bunches of lily of the valley. Single-flower arrangements complemented Vanderbilt's innovative and exuberant interiors and her vibrantly creative lifestyle. ❧

*To be happy—
one must find
one's bliss.*

GLORIA VANDERBILT

MUSE

Gloria Vanderbilt

One of the goals of life is to try and be in touch with one's most personal themes—the values, the ideas, styles, colors that are the touchstones of one's own individual life, its real texture and substance.

OF THE MANY GLORIOUS rooms Gloria Vanderbilt (1924–2019) created for herself and her family, the most famous of them—her patchwork-quilt-covered bedroom—seems a fitting metaphor for her life. Vanderbilt covered every inch of the walls, ceiling, and floors in patchwork, creating a patterned cocoon. She cut and arranged each piece of fabric for the floor herself and sealed it with several coats of lacquer. She left the quilt-cum-curtains unlined so that sunlight could filter through the colored shapes like stained glass. Onto this canvas, she layered additional textures and patterns, including her own collages of an Elizabethan woman and a cavalier, made from fabric scraps and aluminum foil. Using handmade quilts, the quintessential American folk art, Vanderbilt created a magically transporting space, one that conjured Russian dachas, Eastern tented palaces, and a rich, romantic past that never existed. Throughout her life, with her optimism and her art, Vanderbilt combined incongruous parts into a unique, vibrant, and original whole.

It was indeed her talent and energy that she used to piece together a rich, diverse tapestry of a life: a model starting at age fifteen, an actress on stage and screen, a poet, a playwright, a well-regarded

PRECEDING PAGES *Gloria Vanderbilt, 1975.* LEFT *Gloria Vanderbilt,* Geranium, 2006. OPPOSITE *These full-blown tulips remind me of Vanderbilt's fabric for Bloomcraft—famous in the 1970s.*

best-selling writer, a fashion designer who created a sensation with her designer jeans, and an entrepreneur who used herself to market her brand and was among the first to license her name to an array of products. And always and predominantly, Vanderbilt was an artist, whether creating rooms, fabrics, collages, or paintings in a style all her own but that invoked aspects of Chagall, Matisse, outsider art, and the art of Byzantium.

She filled all of her homes with color, pattern, flowers, and a strong sense of what was lacking in her childhood, love. Vanderbilt used flowers—in her paintings, fabric designs, and her arrangements—not in a botanical or horticultural way, but as elements of color and pattern that could enliven and brighten the world. Cut flowers were used to highlight aspects of a room, to pick out certain colors or textures and, if she happened to be photographed in that room, to coordinate with herself and her clothing as well. Yes, she even matched the flowers to herself, but mind you, never in a silly way; always in a clever and exceedingly lovely way. There are several photographs by Horst in which you can see this: Vanderbilt swathed in a pink silk shawl with pink flowers nearby, accenting the pink in the floral fabric covering the sofa on which she lounges, or in a shot of her with her youngest sons in bed, where burgundy and white tulips mirror the burgundy of the boys' silk pajamas and the white of her own silk dressing gown, and echo those hues in the wallpaper. In Vanderbilt's world, it was as if everything could be knitted together, and made beautiful and cozy and whole. ❧

CHAPTER 5

White

*I don't want to boast in advance about my grey, green and
white garden. It may be a terrible failure. I wanted
only to suggest that such experiments are worth trying,
and that you can adapt them to your own taste.*

VITA SACKVILLE-WEST

WHITE-AND-GREEN ARRANGEMENTS are my hands-down favorites—well, maybe second to my roses. They are subtle, quiet, and somewhat ethereal. From the robust petals of tulips, hyacinth, lilies, and tuberose, the delicate and diaphanous cosmos and poppies, towering stems of foxglove, branches of mock orange, the fragile and fragrant gardenia and lilac: how could white not be on everyone's radar? The simplicity of a single Casa Blanca lily, a bouquet of white roses, or a massive froth of baby's breath all have their moment in a powder room, a bedside, or an entry.

I understand that, if the scheme of a room is saturated and rich with textures, white might feel anemic and get totally lost. Pastels and pale muted palettes, shades of beige and, naturally, all-white rooms might be the better partner for your all-white creation. Karen Blixen understood the meaning of nuance when she created huge bouquets of white flowers with just subtle variations in hue, texture, and shape.

So, as the story goes, do as you please. Forget anything and everything anyone has ever said to you about the what, the how, and the where of arranging. Feel free to experiment with material, palettes, locations, and containers. Who are you trying to please, anyway? ❧

MUSE
Karen Blixen

*Flowers in themselves are one
of life's miracles, and it is a delight
to occupy oneself with them.*

WHEN ONE THINKS of Karen Blixen (1885–1962), whose book *Out of Africa* memorialized her years as an expatriate in British East Africa, one's mind does not immediately go to flowers. And yet, flowers, and the arranging of them, were essential to her identity.

Her African residency lasted seventeen years, but the rest of her life, both before and after, was spent at Rungstedlund, her family's manor house north of Copenhagen. Blixen suffered physical ailments for most of her life, so entertaining at home was vital to her. When guests were expected, she would often go into the flower garden in the very early morning in her nightdress and a pair of wellies, and pick armloads of flowers. After dropping them into buckets of water, she would head back to bed. Blixen wouldn't just make an arrangement or two. In order to enchant her visitors, she would festoon every room in the house with extravagant displays. She could devote two or more days to these floral preparations.

The range of Blixen's floral artistry was great— from vases of just one type of flower to mad celebrations of color darting every which way. Like Constance Spry, of whom she was very likely aware, Blixen often employed cabbage leaves, leek foliage, and contributions from the side of the road in her own deeply elegant arrangements. But her work is not imitative; it possesses a pathos all her own, perhaps born of her own difficulties, that seems to signal how

tragically brief moments of true beauty are. Among the most magnificent of her floral work, which has come to us through photographs, are arrangements in richly nuanced monochrome. Blixen was a proponent of defoliating her flower stems, often completely, until sometimes the inflorescences looked like something new entirely. Pristine white tulips denuded of leaves seem to pirouette like slender-legged ballerinas. Set in a delicate opaline vase and placed in front of a pale blue wall, the arrangement calls to mind the restrained boldness of a Balenciaga silhouette. There is a glorious masterpiece of an arrangement of all-white flowers—roses, astrantia, ground elder, hosta flower, and marguerites—but in which the subtle variations of the hues (whites with hints of pink or lilac or yellow) create a painterly effect. One of the most surprisingly beautiful arrangements employs just yellow and black tulips creating a scene that conjures ancient Persia or precious gemstones.

Blixen always knew she was an artist, originally wanting to be a painter. When back at home in Denmark, she began to channel her artistry into words, and she began to arrange flowers. She approached it with the same seriousness, attending to color and composition, just as she did her paintings. "It is," she said of arranging, "as if you are painting a flower picture." Searching for the exact hue an arrangement might be lacking, she was known to hop on her bicycle to scour roadsides or turn up unannounced at the gardens of friends to see if their garden might supply the precise shade needed.

This crafting of flowers into arrangements of great magnificence and originality, for others to admire and comment on, was in keeping with her crafting of her persona as grand and eccentric—she was known to eat only oysters and grapes and drink only Champagne—but also an antidote to it. Flowers were a way for her, as a woman who was known to be quite difficult, to connect with people. Blixen's arrangements were floral offerings of beauty and generosity to those who came to see her. ❧

PAGE 132 Among the most magnificent of Blixen's floral work are arrangements in richly nuanced monochrome. PRECEDING PAGE Karen Blixen, ca. 1955. OPPOSITE White flowers, whatever they are, have a quiet, obliging way of suiting any container that holds them. I find them very pleasing in vessels ranging from humble baskets to sterling silver.

*Don't let anything in the garden
be wasted, but try to find
someone who would like some flowers.*

KAREN BLIXEN

CHAPTER 6

Mixed Bouquets

*A little girl's sense of color and appreciation
of beauty can be stimulated through flowers.*

JACQUELINE KENNEDY

I GUESS IT IS SAFE to say that the majority of what we call floral arrangements are mixed bouquets. A few of these, a few of those, and oh yes, a couple of those, please.

There is no magical formula, ratio, or road map for creating a mixed bouquet and that's what we love about this style of arranging; it is completely open-minded! Imagine creating a miniature version of a painterly, expressive Gertrude Jekyll garden in a vase. Flowers grow at different heights, so try maintaining those levels in your arrangement. A garden has a multitude of varieties, so your composition can too! Mix it up. Let the delphinium and stock stand tall; the ivy will drape itself over the edge; and hardy leaves such as hosta can provide a collar to support less stalwart flowers.

What to select? Where to place? How many? What container should I use? Is this combination too tall . . . too stingy . . . too tight? I understand all of these questions and how many decisions accompany the making of one arrangement. Seriously, it does sound somewhat like prep for a big exam, but trust me (famous last words): with practice and more practice it begins to happen seamlessly, instinctively, unknowingly. The smallest effort will produce results, and the artistic and creative urges you've been storing will soon surprise you. As I have said in previous books, the important thing is just to "give it a go." ❦

Gertrude Jekyll

*The lesson I have thoroughly learnt,
and wish to pass on to others,
is to know the enduring happiness
that the love of a garden gives.*

ARTIST, GARDENER, CRAFTSWOMAN. That was the fitting epitaph Sir Edwin Lutyens engraved on the gravestone of his friend and collaborator Gertrude Jekyll (1843–1932). At seventeen, Jekyll was among the first women to enroll at London's South Kensington School of Art. In London, she attended lectures by John Ruskin, who subsequently praised her paintings, and was inspired by the work of J. M. W. Turner. Informed by her sensibility as a painter and the lessons she learned, Jekyll pioneered a new painterly style of planting—translating the color-blended brushstrokes of Turner into swaths of color and texture using flowers and shrubbery as her subjects. In the Arts and Crafts fashion of the day, Jekyll was also a consummate craftswoman, practicing techniques as varied as embroidery, wood carving, metalwork, gilding, and photography. She was also sought out for her skills in interior decoration. Early on, she exhibited her many talents, but once people began to see the garden she created at her mother's house, her life moved distinctly into the direction of garden design.

As an architect, Lutyens was her perfect partner. Both believed in the ideals of the Arts and Crafts movement, with a high regard for skills and materials in the creation of things both beautiful and useful. Lutyens designed houses from local materials respectful of their settings, and Jekyll made gardens with an equally sympathetic relationship to the house and countryside.

Jekyll considered each plant closely—not just as a spot of color to be carted from the hothouse and popped into the ground, as was the prevailing Victorian style of "bedding out." By making use of each plant's particular culture, habit, color, and foliage, she created schemes that were sophisticated and harmonious—and that changed with the seasons. It is not just the great twentieth-century English gardens, such as Hidcote and Sissinghurst, that are her heirs; our own gardens descend from Jekyll's way of thinking about plants.

Lesser known, perhaps, are her ideas on flower arranging, or "the use of flowers in house decorations," as she termed it, and which she considered as a branch of gardening. In *Flower Decoration in the House* (1907), she gives arranging ideas for every month of the year, even in the dead of winter when one must go poking about in hedgerows for material. She can be prescriptive in ways that feel dated, but given that she was writing in an era when there was a lot of egregious Victorian knickknackery to be railed against, it is understandable. But much of her counsel is timeless: when she writes "a china bowl of lovely roses is for all times an acceptable thing on the table," most of us would still agree. For lunches or dinners, she thinks one can never go wrong with a mix of fruits and flowers: she loved melons and grapes together on a pewter or silver plate, ideally with a trailing strand of clematis or passionflower vine loosely winding amidst them. When she couldn't find vessels to suit her needs, she designed a line of her own, and, similarly, when a gathering basket couldn't be found to suit the long-stemmed flowers she liked to cut, she created one.

When we envision Jekyll—heavy in brooding Victorian garb with bespectacled, badly failing eyes—it may be easy to forget what a powerhouse she was. Over the course of her life, she created more than four hundred gardens and wrote thirteen books and more than one thousand magazine articles. And she didn't even begin writing books until she was fifty-five. At age eighty-six, she published forty-three articles! At the core of all her work is observation, appreciation, and, really, love. "Take any flower you please," she wrote, "and look it over and turn it about and smell it and feel it . . . this is how to make friends with plants, and very good friends." ❧

PAGE 146 *Gertrude Jekyll, ca. 1901.* PRECEDING PAGE *English roses named after Jekyll.* OPPOSITE *A tower of flowers, a colorful bouquet version of the masterful herbaceous borders Jekyll was famous for.*

CHAPTER 7

Greens & Things

*I take green to be not only the predominant color of
a flourishing garden but the emblem of its aspiration, the
barometer of its health, the very mirror of its finish.*

ROBERT DASH, *Notes from Madoo*

I THINK GREEN, LIKE A steady boyfriend, is often taken for granted in a garden. It's the most widespread color—and expressed in a range of hues—in an outdoor environment. The luminescence of leaves that have a way of attracting a single ray of light even on a gray day; the nuanced textures that beg for you to touch them. A cluster of leaves makes a fine arrangement, and green flowers are in a class of their own. Viburnums, hellebores, nicotiana, euphorbias, lady's mantle, amaranth, and spring green tulips are among the inspired flowers that have adopted the palette of leaves. Each of them adds something special to any arrangement of colorful blossoms and, of course, makes a singular statement in a tight bouquet all by themselves.

Some may see green as the supporting cast of characters secondary to the marquee-grabbing leading ladies of summer stock. The blowsy peonies, per-fumed floribundas, slender delphiniums, and robust dahlias—we love them all, but the loyal green of foliage comes first in my garden book. When Fleur Cowles discusses the green of foliage, she admonishes those who think green is a filler. Cowles felt that foliage can boost posies that needed to realize their full potential. In fact, she was known to combine paper flowers with real leaves in an arrangement.

I remember visiting Cowles years ago at her home in London. We sat in the pink salon under the Hessian panels painted by Federico Pallavicini. After a while, I noticed on the opposite side of the room the largest dried cow parsley I had ever seen. I had seen enormous stems along the road in the English countryside, but never anything this size. I left the apartment that day thinking that Cowles had worked a little of her magical realism on this stem pretending to be a tree.

Foliage plants give flower arrangements variety, body, luxuriousness, and moral support. The variation in colors, textures, and sizes make you take a closer look. The silvery green of licorice plant, the chartreuse of lady's mantle, and the dark waxy leaves of camellia foliage can all be counted on to add a spark of light, a little frothiness, or a dash of drama. The leaves of mint, scented geranium, and tomatoes, as well as sprigs of rosemary, offer the added bonus of fragrance that, once encouraged with a slight pinch, will perfume the air.

Philosophically, I think green is the color of our future. Soothing and cool, nurturing, grounded and reassuring, there's something about green that always has me wanting to get to know it better. ❧

The awareness of nature is a gift.

BUNNY MELLON, *Garden Secrets of Bunny Mellon*

MUSE

Fleur Cowles

Unleash your imagination.

THE LEGENDARY EDITOR and society figure Fleur Cowles (1908–2009) was as cheeky and iconoclastic in the way she used flowers as she was in every other aspect of her long and remarkable life. A painter, writer, editor, and diplomatic envoy, Cowles is best known for creating one of the most innovative—and financially extravagant—magazines ever published. *Flair*, which lasted only a year beginning in 1950, featured contributions by the likes of Pablo Picasso, W. H. Auden, Salvador Dalí, and Winston Churchill on pages that popped up, folded out, and were removable, in an array of paper stocks. Cowles's similarly fearless and original style of entertaining, which employed all manner of unusual plants and vessels in a range of floral styles, delighted her often famous guests. (She counted the Queen Mother as her best friend.) In Cowles's illustrious "set" at Albany, as the apartments at this chicest of London addresses are called, flowers were always displayed against the Wedgwood-blue walls. Cowles adored the wildness of weeds in nature, and would display huge arrangements of dried specimens in her rooms, in addition to cultivating them in her garden.

Cowles bristled at the conventions and so-called rules of good-taste flower arranging, such as the long-forgotten principle that flowers must have enough space between them for a butterfly to pass or the dictum that baby's breath must never be used in combination with roses. To Cowles, such snobbery bred conformity and inhibited the freedom to play,

PRECEDING PAGES *Fleur Cowles, 2003.*
LEFT *Fleur Cowles,* Flower Garden, *1972.*
OPPOSITE *Queen Anne's lace will always*
remind me of the giant dried blossoms of
cow parsley in Cowles's London apartment.

which was a hallmark of her style. Cowles adored roses—she dedicated an entire issue of *Flair* to them and she often painted them in her naive, bright, and singular style. She also loved to mix them with baby's breath. Another favorite combination was red roses and pink clover, the weed one finds growing in lawns. Her arrangements could be incredibly modern, almost abstract in design, and also naturalistically abundant and loose, as the occasion or location demanded. When she was entertaining, her centerpieces often had a sly sense of humor. She might combine broccoli with chrysanthemums, or use a watermelon with its center scooped out to hold sweet peas, or pile a large silver platter with a mountain of shelled peas and edge them with just the heads of white roses! As for the treasures she gathered on country roadsides, such as buttercups and daisies, Cowles thought

they were best "accommodated (not arranged)" in a vase or cachepot. Or in another of her delightful turns of phrase, she liked wildflowers "plunked as picked," so that they retained their innocent charms.

Her open-minded approach extended to vessels. While she loved Venetian glass and fine ormolu, every kitchen item with some kind of hole in it was fair game: cake molds, jugs, ginger jars, tea pots with cracked spouts, spice boxes, and of course, every kind of drinking glass. What you would toss, she would have you keep—those tiny hotel jam jars, plastic containers, and soup cans—so that you could paint them or cover them with leaves or stuff them into baskets.

While Cowles eschewed rules, she did offer a few anti-rule rules of her own: *Liberate your imagination*; *Follow your intuition*; *Don't be inhibited*; and my favorite, *Improvise, improvise!* ❧

CHAPTER 8

Baskets

*Baskets are like a sylvan cousin to the
floral arrangement, the one evoking the woods,
the other evoking the field.*

DEBORAH NEEDLEMAN

SHAKER BASKETS, THE NANTUCKET variety, antique Japanese containers, sweetgrass baskets from South Carolina, classic ones from the many regions of France, large woven saucers from Africa, and those previously owned by other collectors—all of these magnificent handmade objects make up part of my collection. To hold them, to inspect them, their histories are almost palpable.

Made from different natural materials—willow, grasses, wisteria, straw, pine, and rattan, to name a few—and boasting myriad shapes, each one has a personality that almost wants to tell you what flower it would most like to hold.

To accommodate my growing collection of baskets in East Hampton, I have added two rows of bronze curtain rods to the ceiling of my flower room and have hung S-hooks from them. The hanging baskets are now all visible and accessible. Editing is key: as new ones are added, some, past their prime, must be retired, always a sentimental moment.

Every basket needs a liner, preferably lightweight. Evian bottles large and small, pickle jars, plastic butter and yogurt tubs—all find a new life in the

flower room, lining baskets. Long before I started collecting baskets, I adopted the practice of lining my antique vases and anything that needed protecting or that had a hairline crack, which would leak slowly over time. Most antiques dealers and designers will attest to falling in love with a vase, ignoring its flaws because they just "had to have it." But anyone who has ever wandered into the dining room or front hall in the morning only to see a river on the table owing to an unnoticeable crack will tell you that that was the *last* time it was going to happen.

In caring for your baskets, it is best to adopt the practice used to keep wicker furniture in good shape—give them a bath. Spray them with the garden hose, immerse them in a tub, and allow them to dry naturally before using again. This simple practice will ensure a long life. Outside Bunny Mellon's basket house at her Oak Spring estate, there is a small square pool that she used for bathing objects in her collection. Practical and beautiful.

In a world that moves at warp speed, baskets have mystery, romance, and love woven into their being because they are wrought by human hands. ❧

Baskets are just an arrangement of twigs.

DEBORAH NEEDLEMAN

MUSE

Bunny Mellon

[A garden's] greatest reality is not reality, for a garden, hovering always in a state of becoming, sums its own past and its future.

BUNNY MELLON (1910–2014) dedicated most of her long life to the pursuit of beauty and knowledge in the realms of gardens, botany, horticulture, and design. But it was for gardens that she reserved her deepest passion.

Born into a pharmaceutical fortune, and later marrying Paul Mellon, one of the wealthiest men in America, Mellon possessed the means to pursue her dreams at the highest level, but so too did she possess the ineffable magic that is the essence of great and original taste. She had an exacting and unerring eye for unexpected combinations. She created compositions of great harmony whether in the layout of a garden or a building, or in the arrangement of objects on a table. Her famous dictum—that nothing should stand out or announce itself at the expense of anything else—meant that "all should give the feeling of calm. When you go away, you should remember only the peace."

It was for this rarefied and understated sensibility that she was called upon by First Lady Jacqueline Kennedy to redesign the Rose Garden at the White House and by Hubert de Givenchy to lay out his garden at the Manoir du Jonchet in the South of France. But this pedigree belies the fact that she was entirely self-taught, her formal schooling having ended at age sixteen. Her garden passion was ignited

in early youth, when at the age of seven, Rachel Lambert—Bunny was a childhood nickname that stuck—created her first garden on the grounds of her parents' estate in Princeton.

Of her many residences, Oak Spring Farm, her two-thousand-acre estate in Upperville, Virginia, was closest to her heart. It was here that she created her paradise from start to finish—house, garden, greenhouses, buildings devoted to potting and to baskets, and a library containing her large and important collection of rare botanical and horticultural books, manuscripts, prints, and illustrations. She lived the last decades of her long life at Oak Spring, where I visited her in what would turn out to be her last interview, at age one hundred.

Oak Spring had been like a siren, calling me—as a decorator, gardener, and book collector—to it. But I am not alone; its rooms and gardens are among the most referenced places in twentieth-century design. Mellon's light touch, in which humble objects live alongside museum-quality masterpieces and everything is given ample space to breathe, shows her great empathy for objects. Mise-en-scènes, such as the enormous sunny yellow-and-orange Rothko that hung above a simple Shaker bench or the small Braque hanging amidst her collection of wicker gardening baskets, have become touchstones of exquisite subtlety. In her well-manicured, painstakingly considered garden, where crab apples are trained to create a tunnel, large trees are clipped into clouds, and herbs are shaped into potted topiaries, her flower beds are full of charm and simplicity. Nothing growing here is of a rare or even unusual variety. Despite

her precision, her artistry keeps everything at Oak Spring entirely unpretentious. During our talk, she shared recollections and a sense of how important gardening was in her life.

"To keep a garden is to create, to care, and to hope," she has written. Mellon took pleasure and comfort from nature, gardens, trees, flowers, and birds, and Oak Spring was a creative laboratory and her refuge from the world. She walked the grounds daily in her Givenchy smock, armed with her wooden clippers always ready to amend and perfect, and she retreated often into the pages of her beloved books. It is perhaps this state of dreaming, planning, and refining, not bound by the past or limited by the present, that is a garden's truest reality and that gave her such solace. "Like a magic carpet," she wrote, "[gardening] has carried me through life's experiences, discoveries, joys, and sorrows." ❧

CHAPTER 9
Roses

I wonder what you would think
of my vases of celery and roses.

BARONESS DE WALDNER

THE MERE MENTION OF ROSES elicits a wide range of reactions and emotions. Clearly, the queen of the flower border, with her captivating feminine ways, has bewitched countless worshippers, well-wishers, and recipients through the ages. The soft, silken blossoms defy the menacing thorns on her long slender neck. Perhaps thorns are symbolic, a desire to not be bothered, as roses and irises alike love to be planted with their kin and greatly benefit from "being alone." Once you have experienced thorns—in fingers, hands, arms, and legs—you will remember that rose long after her blossom has faded and the vase retired to the shelf.

There are those who think roses are the most difficult to grow, the most temperamental member of the flower border. There is no doubt that they require more work, but the benefits to having them are incalculable in my book. I can't imagine "difficult" as a deterrent to a devoted gardener such as C. Z. Guest. While orchids may have been her first passion, she maintained a rose garden of limited choices—following her own advice to keep things simple, and thereby allowing her garden to be her joy, not a chore. Always a delicate balance for enthusiastic gardeners.

There are those of us who take the idiosyncrasies and recalcitrant behavior of a rose in stride, because the end result is worth every prick of her menacing thorns. I appreciate the fact that the personalities of roses are reflected in their postures. Some prefer standing bolt upright; others prefer to be tidy, compact shrubs; some are competitive climbers or errant ramblers. Whatever shape or form, they spell *heaven*.

The delicate creamy clusters of Lykkefund, the deep pink of the high-reaching blossoms of the indomitable America, and the creaminess of the five-petaled Sally Holmes, slightly blushing—each of them create a bouquet with the snip of a single stem.

Their faces have been painted—and are engraved in our memories—by such artists as Fantin-Latour, Redouté, Berjon, Bosschaert, Vallayer-Coster, Isabey, and so many others who were inspired to capture the fleeting beauty of these beguiling, intoxicating, and transient blooms.

The pleasure of growing roses lies in watching Belinda's Dream and Coco Loco change colors, from their deep hues fading to the color of a blushing cheek, and standing under the arbor in the early evening and experiencing the waves of perfume as if someone were standing in the shadows releasing wafts with an atomizer. Nothing, absolutely nothing, is better than putting your nose deep in a blossom to take in every molecule of its ineffable perfume. Just think of Diaghilev's Ballets Russes with Nijinsky dancing *Le Spectre de la Rose*. Captivating. ❦

MUSE
C. Z. Guest

Having a garden is like having a good and loyal friend.

"WHEN I WALK INTO someone's house and see beautiful flowers, it automatically puts me in a good mood," wrote C. Z. Guest (1920–2003) with her typical straightforward aplomb. The blonde-haired, blue-eyed American socialite always had the confidence of her own well-bred convictions. But in the mid 1970s she began sharing them with a wider public through a popular syndicated garden column.

Guest fell in love with plants at a young age. She would constantly badger the gardener in charge of the grounds at her family's estate outside Boston for information. In due time, she was given her own little garden, where she tended corn, beans, lettuce, zinnias, and marigolds. As a young woman, she had a brief rebellious period—performing with the Ziegfeld Follies and having her nude likeness painted by Diego Rivera, before settling down to a more "proper" life. She married Winston Frederick Churchill Guest, second cousin of Winston Churchill, a polo star, and an heir to the Phipps steel fortune.

Her life indeed had the golden halo of privilege. But in 1975, when she was laid up after a riding accident, her friends kept ringing her with their gardening questions. This led to a slender, but optimistic, no-nonsense volume *First Garden* (1976), with an introduction by her friend Truman Capote and illustrations by Cecil Beaton, another friend. Here, Guest offers sweet and encouraging advice for novice gardeners on planting and decorating with flowers, in the hope, she writes, that "you too will feel the same

inspiration I have felt." Despite possessing a larger retinue of garden helpers than most, Guest offers advice quite practicable and adaptable to all situations.

In the garden, it is essential , she says, to simplify: "Don't try to have everything or your garden will quickly become a chore rather than a delight." Even the most experienced gardener would be wise to heed this. She herself had just a rose garden and another for vegetables and cutting flowers. But when it comes to bringing flowers into the house, her advice is to "let your imagination run wild." Guest is generous about sharing her own preferences—an appealing time capsule of late twentieth-century WASP chic. Her favorite summertime colors are orange and yellow; in winter she prefers red and white. She loves roses, but is mad for orchids, and loves cutting and mixing them with other flowers in a vase.

When Guest writes that "last week I discovered a fabulous new arrangement for one room in my house," you know that if it's good, she will repeat it. And with Guest, good has a way of becoming classic.

(Oscar de la Renta recalled her turning up at a formal party wearing a simple cashmere sweater paired with a long satin skirt—a way of dressing that he had never seen before. Simple. Good. Classic.) In the case of this floral arrangement, her discovery was a cluster of humble green zinnias placed in a pair of rare seventeenth-century Chinese porcelain K'ang Hsi frog vessels. She placed the two frogs on either end of a coffee table with a cattleya orchid in the center. And then she scattered a few more orchids and zinnias around the room so that they all "conversed." Chances are good she did not go fussing around for another idea the next time that room needed summer flowers. Other classic Guest suggestions include keeping potted plants on a patio—nothing rare but rather solid, healthy basics, like geranium, hydrangea, daisies, or jasmine. In the bedroom, her preferences run more delicate—a few roses in a vase or a bouquet of violets. For the front hall, Guest loves big plants in baskets—lilies in summer and amaryllis or clivia in winter. Or orchids. Anywhere, at any time. ❧

CHAPTER 10

Blue & White

*I think about making a flower arrangement
the same way I consider doing a room.*

CHARLOTTE MOSS

WHAT IS IT ABOUT THE COMBINATION of blue and white on *anything* that appeals to so many and is a perennial favorite? Schemes with this classic color pairing—Chinese porcelain, delft and Iznik tiles, ceramics from Portugal and Moustiers, layered with Indian paisleys, crisp stripes, checks and ikats—have an inescapably captivating and transporting quality. Blue-and-white ceramics, in a multitude of patterns and motifs, tell stories and, best of all, are available at all price points, making them perfect candidates for vases, cachepots, and jardinières for an endless variety of flowers.

Like a great navy blazer or a crisp white oxford, which are indispensable wardrobe basics, blue-and-white containers are a dependable neutral, a basis for elaborating upon or dressing up. This versatility may explain part of the universal appeal of blue and white. A pair of cachepots on a mantel with tall myrtle topiaries, a low rectangular planter with a bonsai, a delft vase overflowing with tulips, an overscale porcelain fishbowl with floating gardenias, or a Chinese planter filled with orchids—blue and white just works!

*With freedom,
books, flowers,
and the moon,
who could
not be happy?*

OSCAR WILDE

I don't particularly connect Nancy Lancaster with blue-and-white color schemes; I just think of her, like the color combination, as a classic in so many ways: as a Virginian, a style maker, a gardener, and a hostess. The Cecil Beaton photograph of Lancaster—in her Mainbocher dress and jacket, hat cocked just so, standing next to that fabulous Irish Georgian console topped with Chinese vases and a willy-nilly hothouse geranium—is an image that speaks volumes about her. The one item in that photo that struck me the first time I saw it is the ceramic lidded tulipière urn on pedestal, which I imagined was blue and white. I have held that image in my mind's eye for thirty-five years, shopping and scouring markets around the world, and I have never come across one. Never say die. ❧

MUSE

Nancy Lancaster

*Scale is of prime importance,
and I think that oversized scale is
better than undersized scale.*

IT'S NOT JUST BECAUSE we both hail from Virginia
and have a great passion for houses and gardens
that Nancy Lancaster (1897–1994) is included here.
Sharp, confident, witty, and full of natural style—a
woman after my own heart!—it's also that she has
been an inspiration to me for as long as I've been
making houses and gardens. Despite denying that
she was ever a decorator, she is responsible for decorating some of the finest rooms of the twentieth
century. Neither was she a gardener per se, but that
didn't stop David Hicks from referring to her as "the
most influential gardener since Gertrude Jekyll."
Moxie is a fitting adjective for a confident American
beauty with a strong Southern spirit who created the
English country house style—the preeminent style of
a nation other than her own!

Lancaster, who lived most of her adult life in
England, captured the wonderfully disheveled ease
of life in great British country houses, and served
it back to the aristocratic class with an airy dose of
elegance, comfort, and patinated imperfection. As an
American, she saw what was needed to enhance these
houses: she brought in modern plumbing and central
heating to ward against the damp chill and trans-
formed utilitarian bathrooms into cozy places laid
with rugs, lit by fires, and hung with pictures. And
as an upper-class Southerner, she intuitively understood these houses: her own aesthetic was formed by

BLUE & WHITE   211

a romantic nostalgia for run-down plantation houses that had been left to decay following the Civil War, a situation not entirely dissimilar (but without the racial causes) to what was happening with many great houses in postwar Britain.

For her own three English country houses—Ditchley Park in Oxfordshire, Kelmarsh Hall in Northampton-shire, and Haseley Court in Oxfordshire—Lancaster worked first with Sybil Colefax and Stéphane Boudin of Jansen, before partnering with John Fowler and buying Colefax and Fowler in 1944. In each residence, she brought about a welcoming sense of comfort with deep, low sofas and plenty of places to set a drink or a book or even your feet—and always, with good lighting. Every room contained her ideal troika: fire, candlelight, and flowers.

When I made a pilgrimage a few years back to Lancaster's three English homes, I went as much for the gardens as for the houses. I saw how seamlessly she employed the same guiding principles outside in the design of her gardens as she did indoors in her decoration. It was at Haseley Court, with its neglected garden in a terrible state, save for the nine-teenth-century topiary garden of enormous chess pieces that the old gardener continued to lovingly clip every year, where she made her garden masterpiece.

Lancaster's famous sense of scale and of color, always employed with a lightness of touch, can be seen in this garden. She nurtured the giant topiary pieces and left them to work their magic on a huge empty carpet of grass so that the effect was both impressive and delightful. The simple woodwork in the garden—doors, trellises, obelisks, and furniture—was painted the most wonderful shade of blue that is both deep and pale, and ought to be as famous as Jacques Majorelle's blue in Marrakech. In her rooms she always mixed the haute and the humble. Likewise in her gardens, she counterbalanced formality with wildness. Neatly edged borders contained an overflow of floral abun-dance, and manicured areas led out into seemingly uncultivated forest, which of course was as considered as the effortlessness of her decor. In an article I wrote at the time, I noted how Haseley's garden—like all of her houses, with their rooms, furnishings, and vistas—had an atmosphere of invitation at every turn.

To honor Lancaster's influence, we can keep our fires burning, our vases full of blossoms, and we can kick back in a deep, comfortable chair with a good book, and enjoy it all. ❧

PRECEDING PAGES *Nancy Lancaster, 1950s.* OPPOSITE *A bushelful of baby's breath—no longer just an arrangement filler.*

CHAPTER II

Floralscapes

*I have over there a marvelous garden with many
flowers that, for me, offer the best
possible lessons in the composition of colors.*

HENRI MATISSE

EVERY ONCE IN A WHILE—that is, perhaps more times than I care to admit—I might find a small pot or vase that *must* be bought in multiples. I might imagine them lined up on the mantel, at each place setting for a dinner, or perhaps parading down the center of a table. In the summer the nurseries are full of potted possibilities: zinnias, coreopsis, forget-me-nots, marigolds, petunias, and more, no arranging required. You can choose to keep it simple, with one kind of flower, or mix it up and create your own flower border, mixing colors and heights. No rules, countless possibilities.

I have no doubt that in many households similar tabletop experiments have taken place over and over again. Just imagine a long farmhouse table in Tuscany where a collection of terra-cotta pots is filled with olive branches, a grapevine lacing around them. In France, glass bottles might contain fig branches with clusters of fruit at their feet. In America, a group of blanc de chine vases with single branches of white camellia might conjure a Southern landscape down the center of the dinner table. Underlying all of these ideas is improvisation and imagination.

Much has been written about the influence of Pauline de Rothschild's tablescapes with natural elements and objects from the extraordinary trove of Rothschild china. Such arrangements—wild grasses growing out of hills of moss down the center of the table, branches from fruit trees secured in antique Chinese porcelain—were few and far between, or nonexistent, in the Parisian households of her contemporaries. De Rothschild created a sensation and emboldened many to experiment and do the same. I've always thought that these fantastic groupings made so much more sense than a single centerpiece. How often have we been to a table where two people could not see each other over the centerpiece while the rest of the guests had nothing in front of them? It does make sense to spread the beauty and mystery down the center of the entire table, where the eyes of all the guests are treated to your handiwork.

Whether you walk around your own backyard, forage in the local woods, or visit the flower market, the idea is to see the possibilities in things you would ordinarily dismiss. Commonplace plants and objects have a future; they all have the potential to reach new heights in your hands and with your imagination. ❧

MUSE

Pauline de Rothschild

The night before we left we gave a small dinner party in our apartment. The head waitress brought us some frail dark hyacinths, the very first. Just enough for a glass and a few on the tablecloth. Philippe and I will never forget those small sprigs.

A WOMAN OF incomparable originality, taste, and imagination, Pauline Potter de Rothschild (1908–1976) arranged her world with such brilliance that it can be said she turned living into an art. She is renowned for her unconventional way of decorating and entertaining, in particular the marvelous centerpieces she created from weeds, branches, bulbs, and mosses that seemed to sprout directly from the table's surface.

Tall and whippet thin, more striking than conventionally beautiful, de Rothschild had an enchanting, mellifluous voice, that in the words of Valentine Lawford "used to be the prerogative of American women brought up in Italy or France." She was the child of well-born, but badly behaved, Americans living in France, who shunted their young daughter about and neglected her, before shipping her off to America to live as a teenager with relatives in Baltimore. Before her marriage to Baron Philippe de Rothschild, she lived in Paris and New York, where for a time she was a vendeuse for Elsa Schiaparelli and a couture designer for Hattie Carnegie.

*When you take
a flower in your
hand and really
look at it, it's
your world for
the moment.*

GEORGIA O'KEEFFE

At the Rothschilds' Château Mouton in southwestern France, the couple entertained lavishly most evenings, with guests drawn from the realms of art, politics, literature, and science. De Rothschild would begin the day supervising the household activities from her command center in bed. Menus were brought to her, along with a book containing photographs of the house's one hundred eighty dinnerware sets and another containing swatches of the hundreds of tablecloths and napkins she might pair with them. Her full-time flower arranger would then be dispatched with instructions for the day's "landscape table," heading off on a motorized bike outfitted with large pouches to search for branches, berries, heather, or whatever it was that Madame la Baronne had requested. Meals might be set up in any room of the two houses on the property or in any corner of any room. It was said that returning guests would never see the same china, linen, or flowerscape twice.

A dinner in February might boast alder catkins dangling on bare branches rising from a base of dried ferns and oak leaves, as if all had been plucked from a slumbering forest about to wake. Maybe a little later, jonquils might be gathered and arranged as if growing from a bed of moss. These scenes were symphonies of nature, culture, and candlelight. They expressed a kind of reverence for nature that had perhaps more in common with the Japanese art of ikebana than with traditional European centerpieces. They were at once fantastical and humble in their artistry.

Part of what is so remarkable about de Rothschild's style is that her regard for exquisite quality and extravagance was matched in equal measure by her extraordinary restraint. She possessed an unparalleled appreciation of the power of what is not present—what is left out of a scene. In the sitting room of her iconic London flat at Albany, there were no pictures on the walls or rugs on the floor, save for a few bearskins, and what little furniture occupied the space was low and arranged artfully. The room reads more as a work of art than as a place to sit and converse. And indeed, it was a private retreat, for her pleasure alone: she never entertained there, and rarely received visitors. She kept just one set of simple blue-and-white china and in the center of the table, always, a solitary bowl of fruit. This was an extravagance all its own! In her equally famous apartment in Paris, with its walls covered with hand-painted eighteenth-century Chinese wallpaper of blossoming trees and perching birds, as if in an enchanted forest, de Rothschild designed a rolling straw tray that sat only inches off the floor holding a pair of K'ang Hsi vases, each with just a single tall, velvety bearded iris that seemed as if had been plucked from the walls themselves. Through her example, we can see the extravagance of simplicity as much as the luxury of extravagance. ❧

PAGES 224–25 *Pauline de Rothschild, 1969.* PRECEDING PAGES *De Rothschild's still life of K'ang Hsi porcelain and bearded irises on a straw tray extends the imagery of the eighteenth-century Chinese wallpaper.* OPPOSITE *I prefer a single stem of an iris. Some flowers just want to be alone.*

CHAPTER 12

A Single Stem

A flowerless room is a soulless room,
to my way of thinking; but even one solitary little
vase of a living flower may redeem it.

VITA SACKVILLE-WEST

WHEN YOU LOVE FLOWERS, the "less is more" philosophy can be a non-starter. I can't imagine any girl I know telling her boyfriend or partner, "Don't send me a bouquet. Just send me a single stem!" On the other hand, that single stem is an incredibly thoughtful and romantic gesture. I would wager that that single stem does the trick every time.

Elegance is simplicity; simplicity takes courage; courage comes from confidence; and confidence is a prerequisite for style. A single stem is the ultimate in simplicity. When it comes to flower arranging, a single flower, perfectly placed, is a true marker of style and restraint.

There are people who have floral signatures—a single French tulip, an iris, a garden rose, or a stem of tuberose. These flowers become an emblem, a symbol of who they are, a point of view, a personal style. It's not to say they would never have a big bowl of roses or a basket brimming over with hydrangea; it's just that a single element will do, most of the time. I have been in houses where that single blossom seems to fill the room and becomes the focal point. It has a way of drawing you close. Why? Because it is the chosen one, and as a result is surrounded by an air of mystery.

It doesn't matter whether it's your style or a result of your budget, a single blossom can be intriguing. Take a note from Colette, who could write volumes on the beauty, the scent, the essence of a single stem. ❦

GARDENS of the ITALIAN LAKES

FOLLIES of EUROPE   BARLOW · KNOX ·

GUE LIVING COUNTRY, CI

GARDEN

ome Place

MUSE

Colette

*The worrying thing would be if
the future gardens, whose
reality is of no importance,
were beyond my grasp.*

NOVELIST, ESSAYIST, JOURNALIST, photographer, actress, mime, and muse, the thrice-married, many-lovered, Nobel-nominated Sidonie-Gabrielle Colette (1873–1954), better known simply as Colette, was one of the most talented French writers of the twentieth century. Perhaps her best-known work is *Gigi*, for whose Broadway adaptation she discovered Audrey Hepburn, choosing her as the lead. Colette is renowned for mining the pains and pleasures of love; a love that encompassed not just that of the flesh but also that of nature. Her ability to observe and recall and then to transform into miraculous prose the detailed goings-on of the natural world—with its scents, sights, sounds, and textures—was unparalleled. "No one has written better about gardens," said author and activist Germaine Greer.

Colette's self-described idyllic youth in the Burgundian countryside, under the care of a formidable botanizing mother, was what awakened in her a love for the wonders of everything that "germinates, blossoms, or flies." This love fixed itself inside her and fed her deeply throughout her life, but especially in her later years, when she was confined to her Paris apartment with debilitating arthritis. One of her publishers had the brilliant idea to regularly send flowers over to her flat, and should they inspire her, she could write about them, until eventually they would have enough essays for a little book. These essays are collected, along with some others, in a posthumous English-language edition called *Flowers and Fruit* (1986), which I highly suggest you order right away!

Whether describing the conquering strength of a wisteria absorbing an iron railing or beginning an essay on poppies with "So lightheaded!", her words are as light as if carried on the wings of a dove, and yet so dense with earthy revelation. In one of her essays, which I'd like to quote from, she writes in the first person as the proud, arrogant gardenia, self-proclaimed queen of evening-scented white flowers. "Six o'clock . . . Or so claims the white nicotiana," she huffs with disdain. "But the white nicotiana is prone to error. It will be six o'clock when I decree that it is six o'clock. Only then will the terrace, the garden, the entire universe be smothered in my perfume." Thanks to "this feverish mute discourse," as she describes her scent, ". . . the round world reckons one more night of folly." Her vaulted position has but one rival, the tuberose, whose bloom, "fresh as a budding nipple" lasts so long while "three days after I blossom I look like a white kid glove dropped in the gutter."

For those for whom adoration of flowers and the natural world is the closest we come to religion, Colette is our high priestess. Her essays are sonnets to sights that she, trapped indoors, will never see again, and yet they are never mournful. She is thankful to a bunch of fragrant hothouse-forced white hyacinths, swollen and distended from drinking in so much water, "born in a sitz bath shaped like a carafe," because they are able to stand in in her mind's eye for the wild hyacinth or bluebell, that "tall spindly daughter of the woods." Too delicate to survive when picked (and yet tough enough to withstand trampling), it "must be seen only while it lives, and in multitudes, through the still bare copse, and of a blue spread so evenly that from a distance you are deceived: 'Look, a pond . . .'"

Colette could conjure future gardens even if her eyes would never again caress them. Memory, held in her imagination, is not a pale reminder or a sad longing; it is enough, it is complete. In her novel *The Vagabond* (1910), the protagonist realizes she hasn't thought at all about the man she is supposed to marry because instead it's "as if the only urgent thing in the world were my desire to possess through my eyes the marvels of the earth." She goes on to think, what "if indeed that were the only urgent thing? If everything, save that, were merely ashes?" Passions of the flesh, however urgent, pass. Passion for nature remains and sustains. ❧

CHAPTER 13
Floral Arts

*There is no denying
that flowers are my delight.*

COLETTE

FOR CENTURIES, ARTISTS have chosen to capture nature in its glorious and myriad forms, focusing especially on flowers. Their numbers are too numerous, and their techniques and countries of origin too varied, to list them all here. Many artists' iconoclastic, independent, and passionate personalities are the subjects of books well worth exploring. Each volume is not just a biography but also an adventure to some exotic locale, a treacherous terrain, a cottage in the backcountry, or a sheltered and privileged life at court.

For writers, flowers have long been a symbol of optimism and of life. Through the ages they have associated flowers with personality traits, and the Victorians in particular ascribed sentimental meanings to flowers. Ranging from devotion and innocence to good taste, courage, and hope, this symbolic significance enhanced the flower's profile. I think this is a charming Victorian conceit, but the need to upgrade the meaning of a flower escapes me. I prefer to let them *just be*, instead embracing them for their beauty, their fragrance, and the joy that they provide, sans descriptor.

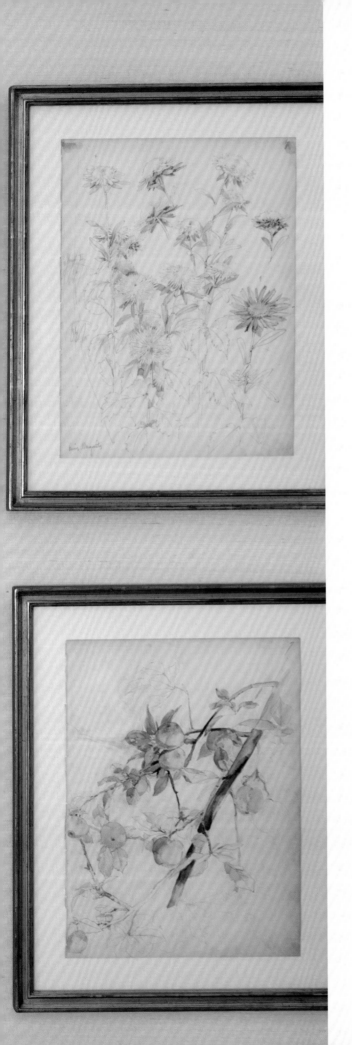

I always think the flowers can see us, and know what we are thinking about.

GEORGE ELIOT

Whether you are a gardener or just a lover of flowers, various art forms featuring flowers bring pleasure year round. Sculptures, paintings, watercolors, and engravings throughout the house create a garden of their own. Bridging the seasons, they provide hope and promise for a flower border to emerge next spring, but most importantly they provide everlasting visual pleasure long after their seasonal cousins have gone to seed.

I owe my own everlasting garden to numerous eighteenth-century artists and engravers; to painters such as Rogers Turner; Anne Messel Parsons, Countess of Rosse; Emma Tennant; Rory McEwen; Katharine Hepburn; Gloria Vanderbilt; and Paula Rubino; as well as to unknown artists whose unsigned portfolios I have purchased over the years. Different styles, techniques, countries, and periods of time—all united with flowers as their muse. ❦

HONEYSUCKLE
Lonicera Periclymenum

Lee Radziwill

Turville was a house of flowers.
When you entered, it had a smell
of straw rugs and burning fires
mixed with the scent of sweet flowers.

CAROLINE LEE BOUVIER RADZIWILL (1933–2019) was known simply as Lee. It was a name that suited her perfectly: precise, direct, unfettered by convention, and without excessive adornment. Radziwill was well known for her unerring eye and elegant, easy style. Whether acting as an American envoy with her sister, Jacqueline Kennedy, in India and Pakistan on behalf of the White House, living abroad in grand style as Princess Radziwill, touring with the Rolling Stones, hanging out with Andy Warhol, or introducing the Maysles brothers to her aunt Edie at Grey Gardens, Radziwill always remained true to her inner compass of style. Nothing she put together was ever too much or, conversely, not enough. This was equally true of her decorating as it was of her sartorial style. The wonderful homes Radziwill made throughout her life were based on principles of tradition, but enriched by her taste for the singular and exotic and buoyed by a breezy, airy lightness that celebrated all things alive and beautiful and flowering.

Radziwill brought a sense of sunlight and the garden into most rooms she made, whether in damp England or on the Upper East Side of Manhattan. It wasn't so much that she was a masterful gardener or an arranger of flowers—although she took pleasure in both—it was that she wanted things to be light, bright, and joyful.

Radziwill described Turville Grange, the manor house in Oxfordshire she shared with her husband Prince Stanislaw Radziwill as "a house of flowers." Every room, she said, "was covered with them." It was the first house on which she collaborated with Renzo Mongiardino, the legendary Italian architect and set designer, and his brilliance with pattern and her passion for flowers made for truly magical rooms. The recipe, if there can be said to be one, often included walls covered in a floral pattern—which went on to extend three-dimensionally into the room on the curtains and onto some of the upholstered furniture—and on which were hung a series of botanical images. (She had a set of eighteenth-century English watercolors and another of nineteenth-century Anglo-Indian paintings that moved with her from house to house.) On the floors would be jardinières and pots, and the tables would boast baskets and vases of plants, flowers, or flowering plants, each chosen to highlight and connect back to a color from the walls.

Radziwill was known also for some extremely dramatic rooms such as the dining room Mongiardino covered with Sicilian scarves onto which artist Lila De Nobili painted vines and blossoms, or the drawing room in which every inch was covered in Indian block-printed fabrics. But she also made other rooms, often painted white, in which sunlight seemed primary. In her last apartment in Paris, the silvery Parisian light bathed the walls and uplifted the space. Here, the roses in Versailles pots on the balcony, the botanicals on the walls, the peony-pink sofa, and the great vases of garden flowers, delivered weekly, were no longer elements tying back into the room, they *were* the room. ❧

PRECEDING PAGES Lee Radziwill, 2013. ABOVE Radziwill's dining room in New York City. OPPOSITE As Radziwill's botanicals followed her from home to home, so will my works by Rogers Turner.

POSTSCRIPT
'til the last petal falls

I HAVEN'T A CLUE how I happened upon a poster of Edward Steichen's *Heavy Roses, Voulangis, France* (1914) in the early 1970s. I do remember being so struck by it that I had to buy it and have it framed for the apartment I shared with three other women my senior year of college. That's another story.

Today, that image is always lurking in my mind when I am in the rose garden or arranging roses or reluctantly plucking faded blossoms from a bouquet. Every once in a while there is one that hasn't quite given up, and so I carefully trim the end of the stem and find a small nosegay or bud vase to give it life support until the last petal falls.

I believe that Steichen's photograph made me think about flowers differently. Once you have made an arrangement, you notice the details and the changes every time you pass it. When you change the water or tidy the stems up, you notice how some blooms have faded and changed color, while others have grown or have expired quickly. Your appreciation for all these nuances will serve you well in the future as you decide what to grow, what to buy, and what and how to arrange.

In the opening pages of my book *Garden Inspirations* (2015), I photographed roses in a state of diminishing voluptuousness similar to those in that poster. I believe that flowers have so much more to say and teach us *after* they've reached their prime. I will savor every last one, until the last petal falls. ❧

from my library

I always felt, in any town,
if I can get to a library, I'll be okay.

MAYA ANGELOU

I REMEMBER MY FIRST visits to the school library: feeling very grown up being with older students, the musty smell of old paper, and the sound of feet shuffling across the floor. Then there was the librarian—the person in the school I thought must be the smartest, the one who had to know everything because you could ask her anything and she knew where to go.

Libraries were a marvel to me then, and today being in my own gives me a sense of calm, where everything is okay. It doesn't matter what I am doing in the library—reading the newspaper or a book or writing a letter—there is a magnetic force imploring me to rediscover something that I have not visited in a long time. This is what libraries do. I have been collecting books for some fifty years. Some come and go, some get gifted or donated, because editing is essential. The most difficult section of the library to purge, outside of first editions and collections of the works of specific writers, is the gardening books. Gardens are about hope. There is always plotting and dreaming to be done for the garden and its flower borders; therefore, research is perennial and books are as necessary as the seeds to be planted. And then there is the wealth of garden writers who amuse, educate, and encourage, as well as share their triumphs and disasters.

Books have always been an amusement, an escape, a reference, and a refuge for me. Included here are some of the books from my garden library that I refer to again and again. Some I may have neglected for a couple of years, others are more regularly consulted, but as Thomas Jefferson said, "I cannot live without books." Agreed! And when I'm in the library I am okay. ❧

BOOKLIST

Here is a sampling of books from my library of flower-related titles. Listings are organized by author, title, and first year of publication. Various versions of each title may be available—many of these books have had several publishers and multiple printings and editions. In some cases, a first-edition copy may be desired; in others, a less-expensive later printing may work just fine. Happy foraging!

A Handbook of Roses Catalogue. David Austin Roses. 1978.

Ackerman, Diane. *Cultivating Delight: A Natural History of My Garden.* 2001.

Alcott, Louisa May. *Flower Fables.* 1855.

Anderson, Alexander Walter. *The Coming of the Flowers.* 1951.

Attlee, Helena. *Italian Gardens: A Cultural History.* 2012.

Bailey, Lee. *Lee Bailey's Small Bouquets: A Gift for All Seasons.* 1990.

Baraton, Alain. *Gardener of Versailles: My Life in the World's Grandest Garden.* 2014.

Beales, Peter. *Classic Roses: An Illustrated Encyclopedia and Grower's Manual of Old Roses, Shrub Roses and Climbers.* 1997.

Beales, Peter. *A Passion for Roses: Peter Beales' Comprehensive Guide to Landscaping with Roses.* 2007.

Beales, Peter. *Roses.* 1992.

Bennett, Sue. *Five Centuries of Women & Gardens.* 2000.

Benzakein, Erin, and Julie Chai. *Floret Farm's Cut Flower Garden: Grow, Harvest, and Arrange Stunning Seasonal Blooms.* 2017.

Berrall, Julia. *A History of Flower Arrangement.* 2000.

Blixen, Karen. *Karen Blixen's Flowers: Nature and Art at Rungstedlund.* 1983.

Bown, Deni. *Alba: The Book of White Flowers.* 1989.

Buchan, Ursula. *Garden People: The Photographs of Valerie Finnis.* 2007.

Burroughs, Laura Lee. *Flower Arranging: A Fascinating Hobby, Vol. 1.* 1940.

Burroughs, Laura Lee. *Flower Arranging: A Fascinating Hobby, Vol. 2.* 1941.

Christopher, Thomas. *In Search of Lost Roses.* 2002.

Chwast, Seymour, and Emily Blair Chewning. *The Illustrated Flower.* 1977.

Coats, Alice M. *Flowers and Their Histories.* 1956.

Coats, Peter. *Roses.* 1962.

Colette. *Flowers and Fruit.* 1986.

Colette. *For a Flower Album.* 1959.

Connaissance des Arts. *Gardens and Flowers: Their Design and Arrangement.* 1966.

Cowles, Fleur. *Flower Decorations: A New Approach to Arranging Flowers.* 1989.

Cowles, Fleur. *The Life and Times of the Rose: An Essay on Its History with Many of the Author's Own Paintings.* 1992.

Cuthbertson, Yvonne. *Women Gardeners: A History.* 1998.

Darcey, Cheralyn. *Flowerpaedia: 1,000 Flowers and Their Meanings.* 2017.

Dash, Robert. *Notes from Madoo: Making a Garden in the Hamptons.* 2000.

De Bay, Philip, and James Bolton. *Garden Mania: The Ardent Gardener's Compendium of Design and Decoration.* 2000.

De Bourgoing, Catherine. *Jardins Romantiques Français: Du Jardin des Lumieres au Parc Romantique.* 2011.

Deitz, Paula. *Of Gardens: Selected Essays.* 2011.

Dellatore, Carl. *Garden Design Master Class: 100 Lessons from the*

World's Finest Designers on the Art of the Garden. 2020.

Dennison, Matthew. *Behind the Mask: The Life of Vita Sackville-West.* 2015.

Dietz, S. Theresa. *The Complete Language of Flowers: A Definitive and Illustrated History.* 2020.

Duthie, Ruth. *Florists' Flowers and Societies (Shire Garden History).* 1988.

Edgarton, S. C. *The Flower Vase: Containing the Language of Flowers and Their Poetic Sentiments.* 1844.

Elizabeth, Charlotte. *Chapters on Flowers.* 1841.

Elizabeth, Charlotte. *Floral Biography: Or, Chapters on Flowers.* 1840.

Elliott, Charles. *The Royal Horticultural Society Treasury of Garden Writing.* 2005.

Elliott, Charles. *This Is the Garden: An Anthology.* 2011.

Field, Ann, and Gretchen Scoble. *The Meaning of Flowers: Myth, Language & Lore.* 2014.

Flowers of Ten Centuries: Catalogue of an Exhibition (April 28– July 26, 1947). 1947.

Frohman, Louis H., and Jean Elliot. *A Pictorial Guide to American Gardens.* 1960.

Galbally, John, and Eileen Galbally. *Carnations and Pinks for Garden and Greenhouse: Their True History and Complete Cultivation.* 2003.

Garmey, Jane. *The Writer in the Garden.* 1999.

Geall, Christin. *Cultivated: The Elements of Floral Style.* 2020.

Genders, Roy. *Anemones.* 1956.

Genders, Roy. *The Cottage Garden and the Old-Fashioned Flowers.* 1969.

Gilmour, John Scott Lennox. *British Botanists.* 1944.

Glenny, George. *Glenny's Handbook to the Flower Garden and Greenhouse.* 1850.

Grace of Monaco (Princess), and Gwen Robyns. *My Book of Flowers.* 1980.

Guest, C. Z. *First Garden.* 1976.

Halsham, John. *Every Man's Book of Garden Flowers: With Short Directions for Their Culture.* 1916.

Hardouin-Fugier, Elisabeth, and Etienne Grafe. *French Flower Painters of the 19th Century: A Dictionary.* 1989.

Heilmeyer, Marina. *The Language of Flowers.* 2001.

Hersey, Jean. *Wild Flowers to Know and Grow.* 1964.

Hicks, David. *The David Hicks Book of Flower Arranging.* 1976.

Hoblyn, Alison. *Green Flowers: Unexpected Beauty for the Garden, Container or Vase.* 2009.

Holland, Leicester Bodine. *The Garden Bluebook: A Manual of the Perennial Garden.* 2012.

Holmes, Eber. *Rose Garden Primer.* 1930.

Horwood, Catherine. *Gardening Women: Their Stories From 1600 to the Present.* 2010.

Hyatt, Brenda. *Primroses and Auriculas.* 1989.

Jekyll, Gertrude. *Flower Decoration in the House.* 1907.

Johnson, Lady Bird, and Carlton B. Lees. *Wildflowers Across America.* 1988.

King, Francis. *The Flower Garden Day by Day.* 1927.

Lack, Walter H. *Florilegium Imperiale: Botanical Illustrations for Francis I of Austria.* 2006.

Lewis, Philippa. *Everything You Can Do in the Garden Without Actually Gardening.* 2009.

Longshore, Lydia, and Southern Accents Magazine. *The Southern Garden.* 2001.

Lowery, Gregg, and Phillip Robinson. *Book of Roses.* 2006.

Macoboy, Stirling. *The Ultimate Rose Book.* 1993.

Masson, Charles. *The Flowers of La Grenouille.* 1994.

Mawson, Timothy. *The Garden Room: Bringing Nature Indoors.* 1994.

McFarland, John Horace. *Memoirs of a Rose Man: Tales from Breeze Hill*. 1949.

McFarland, John Horace. *Roses of the World in Color*. 1936.

McMahon, Bernard. *The American Gardener's Calendar: Adapted to the Climates and Seasons of the United States* (1806). 2008.

Merrick, Amy. *On Flowers: Lessons from an Accidental Florist*. 2019.

Moody, Mary. *Flowers by Color: A Complete Guide to Over 1,000 Popular Garden Flowers*. 1990.

Moss, Charlotte. *Charlotte Moss: Garden Inspirations*. 2015.

Moss, Charlotte. *The Poetry of Home*. 2004.

Nichols, Beverley. *The Art of Flower Arrangement*. 1967.

Nichols, Beverley. *Garden Open Today*. 2009.

Nicholson, Phyllis. *Country Bouquet*. 1947.

O'Byrne, Chris. *Bouquets Insolites*. 1997.

Old Fashioned Roses Catalogue. 1932.

Osler, Mirabel. *A Gentle Plea for Chaos: The Enchantment of Gardening*. 1989.

Othoniel, Jean-Michel. *The Secret Language of Flowers: Notes on the Hidden Meanings of the Louvre's Flowers*. 2019.

Pauwels, Jo. *Jardins Intemporels*. 2003.

Pavord, Anna. *The Tulip: The Story of a Flower That Has Made Men Mad*. 2014.

Pejrone, Paolo. *Private Italian Gardens*. 2017.

Pereire, Anita, and Gabrielle van Zuylen. *Gardens of France*. 1983.

Phillips, Alfred A. *The Bouquet for 1847: Beautifully Embellished*. 1847.

Phillips, Alfred A. *The Moss Rose*. 1848.

Pratt, Anne. *Flowers and Their Associations*. 1840.

Prior, W. D. *Roses and Their Culture*. 1878.

Puttock, A. G. *Primulas*. 1957.

Quackenbush, Alice T. A. *Perennials of Flowerland*. 1929.

Raphael, Sandra. *An Oak Spring Pomona: A Selection of the Rare Books on Fruit in the Oak Spring Library*. 1990.

Ray, Mary Helen, and Robert P. Nicholls. *The Traveler's Guide to American Gardens*. 1988.

Reddell, Rayford C. *A Year in the Life of a Rose: A Guide to Growing Roses from Coast to Coast*. 1996.

Renaud, Philippe, and Marion Faver. *L'Art Floral (Bouquets d'Artistes)*. 1997.

Richardson, Tim. *Great Gardens of America*. 2009.

Rickett, Harold William. *Wild Flowers of the United States, Vol. 1: The Northeastern States*. 1966.

Rickett, Harold William. *Wild Flowers of the United States, Vol. 2: The Northeastern States*. 1966.

Roberts, Harry. *The Book of Old-Fashioned Flowers and Other Plants Which Thrive in the Open-Air of England*. 1901.

Sackville-West, V. *A Joy of Gardening*. 1958.

Sackville-West, V. *V. Sackville-West's Garden Book*. 1968.

Sackville-West, Vita, and Sarah Raven. *Sissinghurst: Vita Sackville-West and the Creation of a Garden*. 2014.

Saunders, Gill. *Ehret's Flowering Plants (The Victoria & Albert Natural History Illustrators)*. 1987.

Scanniello, Stephen. *Easy Care Roses: Low Maintenance Charmers*. 1995.

Scanniello, Stephen. *Jackson & Perkins Rose Companions: Growing Annuals, Perennials, Bulbs, Shrubs, and Vines with Roses*. 2005.

Scanniello, Stephen. *A Year of Roses*. 2006.

Scanniello, Stephen, and Tania Bayard. *Climbing Roses*. 1994.

Scanniello, Stephen, and Tania Bayard. *Roses of America*. 1990

Scanniello, Stephen, and Douglas Brenner. *A Rose by Any Name: The*

Little-Known Lore and Deep-Rooted History of Rose Names. 2009.

Scott-James, Anne. *Down to Earth*. 1998.

Segal, Sam. *Belief in Nature: Flowers with a Message*. 2012.

Shephard, Sue. *The Surprising Life of Constance Spry: From Social Reformer to Society Florist*. 2011.

Shewell-Cooper, W. E. *The Complete Flower Grower*. 1964.

Sitwell, Sacheverell. *Old Fashioned Flowers*. 1939.

Smith, Clinton. *Veranda: The Romance of Flowers*. 2015.

Spry, Constance. *Come into the Garden, Cook*. 1943.

Spry, Constance. *Flower Decoration*. 1934.

Spry, Constance. *How to Do the Flowers*. 1954.

Steen, Nancy. *The Charm of Old Roses*. 1987.

Steinmeyer, James M. *Northern European Garden Pavilions: Watercolors, 2001*. 2001.

Stewart, Martha, and Kevin Sharkey. *Martha's Flowers: A Practical Guide to Growing, Gathering, and Enjoying*. 2018.

Stone, Doris M. *The Great Public Gardens of the Eastern United States*. 1982.

Tanase, Nicolae. *The Language of Flowers: The Dictionary of Flowers and Their Beautiful Timeless Meanings*. 2019.

Tankard, Judith B. *Gertrude Jekyll and the Country House Garden: From the Archives of Country Life*. 2011.

Thomas, Graham Stuart. *Climbing Roses Old and New*. 1983.

Tomasi, Lucia Tongiorgi. *An Oak Spring Flora: Flower Illustration from the Fifteenth Century to the Present Time: A Selection of the Rare Books, Manuscripts, and Works of Art in the Collection of Rachel Lambert Mellon*. 1997.

Tomasi, Lucia Tongiorgi, and Tony Willis. *An Oak Spring Herbaria: Herbs and Herbals from the Fourteenth to the Nineteenth Centuries*. 2019.

Trovillion, Hal W. *Flowers from Old Gardens: A Selection of Old and Rare Garden Sentiments*. 1951.

Tyler-Whittle, Michael Sidney, William Curtis, and Christopher D. K. Cook. *Curtis's Flower Garden Displayed: 120 Plates from the Years 1787–1807*. 1981.

Utterback, Christine. *The Serious Gardener: Reliable Roses*. 1997.

Verey, Rosemary, and Ellen Samuels. *The American Woman's Garden*. 1984.

Waterfield, Margaret H. *Garden Colour: Spring, by Mrs. C.W. Earle; Summer, by E.V.B.; Autumn, by Rose Kingsley; Winter, by the Hon. Vicary Gibbs*. 1922.

Watters, Sam. *American Gardens, 1890–1930: Northeast, Mid-Atlantic, and Midwest Regions (Urban and Suburban Domestic Architecture)*. 2006.

Way, Twigs. *Virgins, Weeders, and Queens: A History of Women in the Garden*. 2006.

Westcott, Cynthia. *Anyone Can Grow Roses: The Plant Doctor's Rose Book*. 1952.

Williams, Dorothy Hunt. *Historic Virginia Gardens: Preservations by the Garden Club of Virginia*. 1975.

Wilson, Helen Van Pelt. *Climbing Roses*. 1955.

Wright, Richardson Little. *The Practical Book of Outdoor Flowers*. 1924.

Wright, Richardson Little. *A Small House and Large Garden*. 1924.

RESOURCES

England

Colefax & Fowler
Antiques, accessories, and vases
sibylcolefax.com

Garden Museum
Accessories and gifts
gardenmuseum.org.uk

Guinevere Antiques Ltd
Antique furniture and accessories
guinevere.co.uk

Julia Boston Antiques
Ceramics and antiques
juliaboston.com

Nina Campbell
China, glassware, and furniture
ninacampbell.com

OKA
Accessories, faux flowers, and furniture
oka.com/shops

Robert Kime
Antiques and furniture
robertkime.com

Tate Modern Gift Shop
tate.org.uk/

France

Astier de Villatte
Ceramics, accessories, and scented candles
astierdevillatte.com/shop
(also available at US stores)

Au Bain Marie
Antiques, china, and accessories
aubainmarie.fr/en/

Le Cabinet de Porcelaine
Porcelain objets and flowers
lecabinetdeporcelaine.com

Carmen Almon
Botanical art and flowers created from copper and brass
carmenalmon.com/garden-flowers

La Tuile à Loup
French ceramics, aptware, and baskets
@latuilealoup

United States

And George
Antiques and accessories
andgeorge.com

Annette La Velle Antiques
Antiques
lindenlaanantiques.com

The Antique and Artisan Gallery
Antiques, furniture, and accessories
theantiqueandartisangallery.com

Antiques & Interiors at the Pavilion
An antiques collective
(713) 520-9755

Antiques of South Windermere
Seventeen South Antiques
Antiques and accessories
antiquescharleston.com

Avala Inc.
Porcelain and accessories
avalainc.com

Avery & Dash Collections
An antiques collective
averydash.com

Bardith, Ltd.
Antiques, china, and porcelain
bardith.com

Caroline Faison Antiques
Antiques and ceramics
daltonbain.com/carolinefaison/

Casa Gusto
Antiques, papier-mâché, painted furniture, and ceramics
getthegusto.com

Chateau Domingue
Architectural antiques, garden ornaments, and furniture
chateaudomingue.com

Circa
Decorative accessories
circainc.com

Clare Potter
Custom porcelain flowers
clarepotter.com

Coco & Dash
Furniture and decorative accessories
cocoanddash.com

Comer & Co.
Antiques and accessories
comerandco.com

Dixon Rye
Furniture and accessories
dixonrye.com

Dutch Flower Line
Flowers
dutchflowerline.com

Found
Antiques and accessories
foundforthehome.com

Frances Palmer Pottery
Ceramics and vases
francespalmerpottery.com

Fritz Porter
Antiques, furniture, and textiles
fritzporter.com

G. Page Wholesale Flowers
Flowers
gpage.com

Helen Storey Antiques
Antique furniture and accessories
helenstoreyantiques.com

Holiday Flowers & Plants
Orchids, ferns, trees, and shrubs
holidayflowersnyc.com

Hudson Grace
Accessories and tabletop
hudsongracesf.com

Interiors Market
An antiques collective
interiorsmarket.com

Ivy Nursery
Nursery plants, accessories, and vases
ivynursery.com

Jamali Garden
Garden accessories, vases, cachepots, and accessories
jamaligarden.com

James Friedberg
Glass bottles and vases
jamesfriedberg.com

John Derian
Accessories, ceramics, textiles, and gifts
johnderian.com

Karla Katz Antiques
Antiques and accessories
karlakatz.com

Kenny Ball Antiques
Antiques and accessories
kennyballantiques.com

Kim Faison Antiques
Antiques, delftware, ceramics, and furniture
kimfaisonantiques.com

Kinsey Marable & Co.
Rare books and collections services
privatelibraries.com

KRB
Antiques and accessories
krbnyc.com

Lars Bolander
Antiques and accessories
larsbolander.com

Lexington Gardens
Floral accessories, garden items, and custom dried arrangements
lexingtongardensnyc.com

Lee Stanton
Antiques, furniture, and accessories
leestanton.com

Marston Luce Antiques
Antiques, furniture, and accessories
marstonluce.com

Mecox Gardens
Antique and new furniture and accessories
mecox.com

Meg Braff Designs
Furniture and accessories
megbraffdesigns.com/shop

Monticello Gift Shop
Accessories, garden items, seeds, and vases
monticelloshop.org

Nick Brock Antiques
Furniture and accessories
nickbrockantiques.com

Parc Monceau
Antiques
parcmonceauatl.com

Peachtree Battle Antiques
An antiques collective
peachtreebattleantiques.com

The Pink Door
Antiques and accessories
daltonbain.com/ThePinkDoor/

Plaza Flowers
Flowers and topiary
plazaflowersnyc.com

Sag Harbor Florist
Flowers and plants
sagharborflorist.net

Sue Fisher King
Accessories
suefisherking.com

Terrain
Plants, garden accessories, vases, and gifts
shopterrain.com

Thompson + Hanson
Gifts, plants, accessories, and decor
thompsonhanson.com

Tom Stansbury Antiques
Antiques
tomstansburyantiques.com

Virginia Museum of Fine Arts
vmfashop.com/

Vladimir Kanevsky
Porcelain and tole flowers
thevladimircollection.com

W. Gardner, Ltd.
Antiques and garden accessories
wgardnerltd.com

William Laman
Antiques, garden furniture, planters, and accessories
williamlaman.com

William-Wayne & Co.
Decorative tabletop accessories
william-wayne.com

Wolf Hall Antique Collective
Antiques
wolfhallantiques.com

Wynsum Antiques
Antiques
wynsum.shop

Zezé Flowers
Flowers
@zezeflowers

ACKNOWLEDGMENTS

I AM GRATEFUL, once again, to everyone who works with me for their support and patience, at home and in the office.

To Lisa Stamm for over thirty years of garden guidance and planning, which has helped me establish flower borders that provide limitless joy and flower arrangements for the house.

To Stephen Scanniello for his planning of the rose gardens, for his selections, for hunting down unusual and rare varieties (and their histories), I am deeply grateful, and to the masterful hand of Zach Eannuzi who maintains and trains the roses and weaves them through shrubs and trees, creating surprises everywhere.

To Kimberly Power, my assistant and chief collaborator, who organizes everything, researches photos, manages all manuscript edits, keeps me on track, and so much more.

To Philip Reeser, my editor, for his interminable patience and abundant guidance, and Charles Miers, my publisher, for his intuition and sparks of inspiration.

To Sarah Gifford, my book designer, for her art direction and speedy turnarounds.

To all of the suppliers of beautiful flowers mentioned in my introduction and repeated in the Resources section. Thank you.

To Brittany Ambridge for her beautiful photographs and pleasant demeanor.

To the countless antiques dealers for all of the vases, cachepots, baskets, and jardinières I have purchased over the years. Thank you.

To my stepson James Friedberg for coming on this journey with me and collaborating on a collection of handblown vases that I use again and again. The collection will be available upon publication of this book.

And always, always to Barry for supporting me throughout the process, and who takes as much joy in the results as I do. ❧

271

First published in the United States of America in 2021 by
Rizzoli International Publications, Inc.
300 Park Avenue South
New York, New York 10010
www.rizzoliusa.com

Publisher: Charles Miers
Senior editor: Philip Reeser
Production manager: Kaija Markoe
Design coordinator: Olivia Russin
Copy editor: Victoria Brown
Managing editor: Lynn Scrabis

Design: Sarah Gifford
Project manager: Kimberly Power

ISBN: 978-0-8478-7014-1
Library of Congress Control Number: 2020941330

2021 2022 2023 2024 / 10 9 8 7 6 5 4 3

Printed and bound in Italy

Facebook.com/RizzoliNewYork
Twitter: @Rizzoli_Books
Instagram.com/RizzoliBooks
Instagram.com/CharMossNY
Instagram.com/Charlottemossco
Pinterest.com/RizzoliBooks
Youtube.com/user/RizzoliNY
Issuu.com/Rizzoli

Photography Credits

All images copyright © Charlotte Moss except for those on
the pages listed below:

4, 5, 7, 21 (*top right*), 24, 25, 27, 30, 31, 34–35, 36 (*top right, bottom
right, and bottom left*), 37, 38–39, 40, 41 (*top left and top right*), 42
(*top right and bottom right*), 44–45, 46, 47 (*top right and bottom
left*), 48–49, 50–51, 52, 53, 54, 55, 57, 59, 60, 62, 63, 64, 70–71, 72,
73 (*top right, bottom right, and bottom left*), 74–75, 76, 77 (*top and
bottom*), 78, 79, 81, 91, 94–95, 96–97, 159, 205, 243, 244–45, 248,
249, 252, 254, 255, 259, 262, 270: Brittany Ambridge

12: Collection of Mr. and Mrs. Paul Mellon, National
Gallery of Art

28: Simon Upton, *House & Garden* © Condé Nast

33 (*top right*), 47 (*bottom right*), 112, 113, 231, 251, 253:
Pieter Estersohn

47 (*top left and bottom left*), 56: Jean-Pierre Uys

66–67, 84, 215: Miguel Flores-Vianna

86–87, 98–99, 155, 247, 250 (*bottom right*): Eric Striffler

100–01: Paul Popper / Popperfoto / Getty Images

116–17, 196–97, 222–23: Michael Mundy

118–19: Horst P. Horst / Condé Nast Collection / Getty Images

120: © Gloria Vanderbilt

132 (*top and bottom*): Karen Blixen, *Karen Blixen's Flowers Nature
and Art at Rungstedlund*. Christian Eilers Publishers, 1992.

133: Hulton Archive / Getty Images

146: Heritage Images / Hulton Archive / Getty Images

147 (*top*): REDA&CO / Universal Images Group / Getty Images

147 (*bottom*): Flowerphotos / Universal Images Group /
Getty Images

162–63: Robert Trachtenberg / Trunk Archive

164: © Fleur Cowles

180–81: Fred R. Conrad / *The New York Times*

182–83: Jonathan Becker

184: Michael Dunne, *Architectural Digest* © Condé Nast

198: François Halard, *House & Garden* © Condé Nast

210–11: © The Cecil Beaton Studio Archive at Sotheby's

224–25: Horst P. Horst / Condé Nast Collection / Getty Images

226–27: Horst P. Horst, *Vogue* © Condé Nast

238–39: Reporters Associés / Gamma-Rapho / Getty Images

256–57: © François Halard

258: Derry Moore, *Architectural Digest* © Condé Nast